Books in the
Church's Teachings for a Ch
series include:

Companions on the Episcopal Way

VOLUME 9
in the
Church's Teachings for a Changing World series

STEPHANIE SPELLERS AND ERIC H. F. LAW

 CHURCH
PUBLISHING
INCORPORATED

Church Publishing
19 East 34th Street
New York, NY 10016
www.churchpublishing.org

Cover art: *Supper-at-Emmaus* © 2017 by James He Qi
Cover design by Laurie Klein Westhafer, Bounce Design
Layout and typesetting by Beth Oberholtzer

Library of Congress Cataloging-in-Publication Data

Names: Spellers, Stephanie, author.
Title: Companions on the Episcopal way / Stephanie Spellers and Eric
    H.F. Law.
Description: New York : Church Publishing, 2018. | Series: Church's
    Teaching for a Changing World, VOLUME 9
Identifiers: LCCN 2018006961 (print) | LCCN 2018018074 (ebook) |
    ISBN 9781640650374 (ebook) | ISBN 9781640650367 (pbk.)
Subjects: LCSH: Episcopal Church.
Classification: LCC BX5930.3 (ebook) | LCC BX5930.3 .S64 2018
    (print) | DDC 283/.73—dc23
LC record available at https://lccn.loc.gov/2018006961

Printed in the United States of America

Contents

Preface

This series began as a conversation. We were sitting at the Episcopal Church's General Convention in 2012 with Church Publishing Editorial Director Nancy Bryan, wondering whatever happened to the Church's Teachings Series. That venerable set of books was used and referenced widely throughout the Episcopal Church and had gotten us and our peers through the General Ordination Exams for priesthood. Perhaps the church was due for an update?

We also wondered what would happen if you brought an intentionally intergenerational and multicultural perspective to the basics of Episcopal faith and tradition. The conversation went for hours. The conversation became this series, Church's Teachings for a Changing World.

That spirit of dialogue has guided each volume along the way, and we're grateful for the esteemed partners who were willing to walk with us:

- Volume 1: *The Episcopal Way*—Eric Law and Stephanie Spellers on Episcopal identity and life

- Volume 2: *The Episcopal Story: Birth and Rebirth*—Tom Ferguson on history

- Volume 3: *A Faith for the Future*—Jesse Zink on theology

- Volume 4: *Church Meets World*—Winnie Varghese on contemporary society and justice

- Volume 5: *Formed by Love*—Scott Bader-Saye on ethics

- Volume 6: *Following the Way of Jesus*—Michael Curry on practical ministry, with essays by Megan Castellan (evangelism), Anthony Guillen (multicultural and new ministries), Broderick Greer (racial reconciliation), Kellan Day (young adult ministry), Nora Gallagher (care of creation) and Robert Wright (leadership)

- Volume 7: *A Word to Live By*—Lauren Winner on Scripture

- Volume 8: *Gathered for God*—Jeffrey Lee and Dent Davidson on worship

In this series, we have placed leaders and thinkers in conversation with traditions, Scriptures, experience and reason in the world today. As much as possible, we have opted for language that sounds like regular people who might be talking and walking down the street. That practice came from our shared commitment to allow the Episcopal Way to do what it was born to do: speak of catholic traditions (that is, part of a universal church, one that spans culture, time, region, and perspective) in the vernacular (that is, the spoken, visual, cultural language of a people).

catholic: part of a universal church, one that spans culture, time, region, and perspective

We have sought to place multiple realities side by side, trusting that God will reveal something true and good in the space between if we stay and listen long enough. Ideally, Church's Teachings for a Changing World invites people from a wide range of backgrounds and church experiences into a dynamic conversation about faith, dialogue and the generous give-and-take that makes Episcopal life possible.

vernacular: the spoken, visual, cultural language of a people

We Need to Talk

At the close of the first volume, we expressed this conviction:

> Ultimately, it is not enough to understand the Episcopal Way. If there is one thing we know about being Episcopalian, it is that you have to practice it. And if there is one thing we know about the world today, it is that you cannot wait for someone to enter your church to find out what a great Christian you are. Walking the Episcopal Way has to take you outside.

In this final volume, we pick up where the first one ended—with the belief that the Episcopal Way takes you outside *and* into conversation. So we begin this book by hosting conversations with the series' authors and providing summaries of each volume: history, theology, contemporary society, ethics, practice of ministry, Bible and worship. After these conversations and reflections, we will invite you to take up practices that deepen and expand your own practice of walking and talking the Episcopal Way: with yourself, with God, with your community, with your neighbors, with your "enemy."

Our church and our world need help having those conversations today. In the first volume, we spoke of greater isolation in American life and the need for more intentional presence, online or in person. Today, it seems we are getting even more diverse, and even less capable of relating and appreciating, much less celebrating and loving. Have we forgotten the importance of companionship, relationship, and conversation in Christian life? It is hard to be fully human when we're cut off from each other. It is even more difficult to grow as a Christian in isolation.

To be a Christian in the Episcopal Way is not something you do alone or even in the comfort of your own echo chamber. We need companions—God to love and inspire us, Scripture and tradition to ground us, community to hold and challenge us, diverse neighbors to share in mission, opponents to reveal truths we never would have imagined. All those relationships prepare us to engage a diverse and changing world while staying connected to our identity as Episcopal followers of the God we know in Jesus Christ.

Introduction

The first volume, The Episcopal Way, *opened with a short play about two volunteers at a local soup kitchen: Mark, a college student, and Susan, a long-time Episcopalian. It is now about a month since that conversation . . .*

Mark: Susan. Susan! Where are you going?

Susan: I don't care. Home? Church? Maybe I'll wrap myself in a blanket and binge-watch "Game of Thrones."

Mark: Can I at least walk with you?

Susan: Sure. (*Awkward silence.*) First it was the church shootings in Charleston, and then Sutherland Springs, Texas, and Parkland, Florida. I never thought it would hit us here, in a soup kitchen.

Mark: Maybe I need to get a gun. If I had one, maybe Francisco wouldn't have gotten shot.

Susan: You don't mean that.

Mark: Well then, what do you Episcopalians do at times like these?

Susan: I wish I had the answers.

Mark: Hey, we're passing your church right now. And isn't that Maria?

Maria: You guys look strange. Is everything ok?

Mark: Are you the only one who doesn't know what just happened?

Maria: What? I was working on my sermon earlier. I hated missing the soup kitchen.

Susan: Some guy came in with a gun and shot all these people, including Francisco. He jumped in front of a teenager to protect her from the bullets.

Mark: He's always watching out for everybody else, even though he's a guest himself.

Maria: My God. Is he okay?

Mark: The paramedics took him to the hospital. They said he'll survive.

Maria: I wondered why he wasn't here for Eucharist. He always comes after dinner.

Susan: Mark, you asked what an Episcopalian could do. There are a lot of choices—march, change policy, eliminate the poverty that drives some people to violence—but I know where we have to start.

Mark: What?

Susan: Take communion to Francisco.

Maria: That's a great idea. Follow me inside . . .

Mark: This place is amazing! What's that awesome music?

Maria: Our organist is just practicing.

Mark: All this beauty. It could really change the way you approach the pain of the world. And what's this window? He looks like he's my age.

Maria: This is Jonathan Daniels, a modern-day martyr.

Susan: He was a white young man who left school in New England to join the civil rights struggle in Alabama. He died in 1964 after he pushed a black teenaged girl aside and took a bullet for her.

Mark: I see the message here: "No one has greater love than this, to lay down one's life for one's friends." That's intense.

Susan: Jesus said that.

Maria: And people who follow Jesus like Jonathan Daniels did—they're our saints.

Mark: Why would anybody take a risk like that?

Maria: You heard it: love. It's stronger than death and pain. There's a story about Jesus's followers just after he died. They were walking down the road, upset and heartbroken, when the resurrected Jesus appeared and walked with them. Love brought him back to them, and that loving presence helped them to carry on. He's with us, too.

Mark: How is he "with" people? How is death not the end?

(Maria opens the ambry—a wall-mounted cupboard near the altar—and takes out a container.)

Mark: What's that?

Maria: Reserved sacrament. Bread and wine that we blessed at the table on Sunday. The body and blood of Christ.

Mark: This is getting weird.

Maria: Hang in there. You see, on the night Jesus was handed over to suffering and death, he took bread; and when he had given thanks, he broke it, and gave it to his friends, and said, "Take, eat: This is my Body, which is given for you. Do this for the remembrance of me."

Susan: And after supper he took the cup of wine; and when he had given thanks, he gave it to them, and said, "Drink this, all of you: This is my Blood of the new Covenant, which is shed for you and for all for the forgiveness of sins. Whenever you drink it, do this for the remembrance of me."

Mark: So this is symbolic?

Maria: More than that. We eat this bread and drink this wine. When we do, we've all got Jesus inside us. We're one body, his body. He is alive, and he is with us.

Susan: When one of us is hurting, all of us are hurting.

Mark: This is what Francisco came to church for after he had dinner at the soup kitchen?

Susan: Yes.

Mark: Well, then we should definitely take this to him.

Maria: Which hospital is he in?

Mark: Emmaus Hospital.

Susan: Let's hurry and get there now.

Once upon a time, the followers of Jesus endured a walk a lot like the one Susan and Mark take in this play. Jesus had just been crucified, and they were running scared down the road to Emmaus (Luke 24:13–35). Would they be next? Was there anything to hang onto? Then Jesus showed up. Of course they didn't recognize him at first, but maybe that was okay. It gave them a chance to open up about their confusion, longing, and sense of utter betrayal. It gave them the chance to reach out in authentic openness with a total stranger who was curious and asked wondering questions as he walked with them.

Compare the play to the Luke 24:13–35 account of the disciples' journey down Emmaus Road. What similarities do you notice? What's different?

When they arrived at Emmaus, they invited Jesus to stay and eat with them. That's when their eyes were opened. Jesus had promised he would be known to them in the breaking of the bread, and he kept his promise. They exclaimed to each other, "Were not our hearts burning within us while he was talking to us on the road, while he was opening the scriptures to us?" Then they returned to Jerusalem to join and celebrate with the other disciples.

In the play, Susan, Mark, and Maria come from different pathways to become companions through tragedy and confusion. By walking with each other, sharing their questions and stories—stories of Jesus and the saints, stories of beauty and sacrament—they found the way toward meaning and wholeness. The same brother, friend, and savior who showed up on the Emmaus Road was their companion, too.

The Way of Relationship

Companionship and relationship have been central to Christian life since before there was anything called "Christianity." In the beginning, before the earth was formed, when humanity was less than a dream, there was God. The Father, the Son, and the Holy Spirit; Creator, Redeemer, and Sustainer—these are different sides of God in conversation and relationship with each other. The Father or Creator is the force who holds all of creation and drives all things toward wholeness and justice, and who shows compassion and mercy when we fall down. The Son or Redeemer is the face of God with us; the one who embodies and calls us to a way that is unselfish, loving, free and fearless; the one who eventually dies and rises again in order to draw us into eternal union with the Father and Spirit. The Holy Spirit is the power who extends forth, sustains us, makes us bold, opens new windows onto the truth, and challenges us to embrace and take part in God's new thing. As Stephanie has reflected in other writings:

> The Trinitarian God is a God in *perichoresis*, or an eternal, continual dance, with Godself. The Father embraces the Son who embraces the Holy Spirit who embraces the Father . . . for eternity. The Creator in union with the Redeemer who is in union with the Sustainer who is in union with the Creator . . . at all times and in all places. That relational quality propels God into creation, where God yearns for relationship with us all and draws us beyond our barriers and into relationship with each other.*

Especially in Jesus Christ, God reaches out beyond all alienation and beckons us, "Come, join the dance." He enjoys deep union with the Creator and the Spirit, but he doesn't keep it to himself. When we are in union with him, we enter into the lively dance of the Trinity.

The pattern Jesus sets is a specific one. Any who would follow him must keep reaching and opening. We've got to stay curious about who else God wants to welcome into the dance, even as we enjoy the intimacy and beauty of the existing circle. Relationship with companions is the heart of Christian life and the Episcopal Way.

---

* Stephanie Spellers, *Radical Welcome: Embracing God, The Other, and the Spirit of Transformation* (New York: Church Publishing, 2006), 33.

Just look at the word "companion," and you will see this truth unfolding:

Latin	*com* (together with) + *panis* (bread)
Old French	*compaignon* (one who breaks bread with another)
Middle English	*companion*: one who breaks bread with another or travels with another

Until recently, travel for human beings has been a treacherous venture. You couldn't just set out on your own, or if you did, you were on the lookout for others with whom to travel. With whom would you both navigate the path, identify the next food source, and ward off danger? The idea of managing without a companion would have been laughable even 150 years ago.

That's not true for many people today. Robert Putnam traced the breakdown in human relationship and civic institutions in his book *Bowling Alone*. In America, more and more of us travel alone, eat alone, live alone, surf the web alone, manage death alone. That impulse also shapes American spiritual life: you could affiliate with a particular tradition and a regular gathered community, but why not piece together your own hybrid of beliefs, practices, and circles? Who needs regular companions and partners?

We do, if we hope to experience the fullness of life in Christ. God exists in relationship, and God is known most fully when we are in relationship: with God, with each other, with all of creation. Did you know Episcopal priests aren't allowed to celebrate the Eucharist (also known as Communion) alone? Even the meal where we come to know Jesus, by the power of the Holy Spirit, requires the presence of other people.

Alas, the circle of companions isn't likely to look like what any one of us would choose. Some companions will be friends, some acquaintances, some more like enemies (maybe that's one of the reasons Jesus tells the disciples to love their enemies—it's the only way they will come to see the fullness of all that he is trying to reveal to them).

A companion may be a whole community of people on the way or an institution struggling to be faithful to its call. A companion may be a prayer, a sacred story, or a tradition. Certainly we are companioned by the still small voice of God and the roaring Spirit who stirs and carries us where we dared not go. And Jesus is the ultimate companion: he continues to live and walk among us, guiding us on the journey (one who travels with) and offering himself as bread that sustains us like nothing else (one who breaks bread).

In the second part of this book, we will explore the way of conversation and dialogue with all these companions on the Episcopal Way. For now, we rest with this point: when it comes to Christian faith, especially the Episcopal Way of following Jesus, it's still best not to venture out alone. We walk and break bread with each other—friend, neighbor, community, enemy—in order to fully be with God and to become all that God intends us to be.

PART I

Conversations on the Way

Author Reflections on the Series

Every author who wrote a book for Church's Teachings for a Changing World received a similar charge: "Imagine you're on a train or walking down the street with someone who doesn't know the Episcopal Church. How would you talk with them about the church's (fill in the blank with your topic)?" We asked that question to be sure the tone was accessible and conversational, as if the author really were walking alongside others as both a teacher and a companion.

These books are designed to embody the spirit of conversation and companionship at the heart of the Episcopal Way. It was only right to return to each author for one more conversation, this time using a set of "wondering" questions based on

Learn more at www. godlyplayfoundation.org

1

queries for exploring faith through Godly Play, an inquisitive learning process based on Montessori learning methods. Here are our questions:

- I wonder . . . what part of the book you contributed do you like best?

- I wonder . . . what part of the book is most important to you?

- I wonder . . . what part of the book would you change?

- I wonder . . . what would you highlight from your book if you were in conversation with a younger person or someone new to church or to faith?

Let the conversation continue . . .

Chapter 1

A Conversation on the Episcopal Way with Stephanie Spellers and Eric Law

"Given the changing cultural landscapes within which we live, given that emerging generations and many of our neighbors have little if any affinity for Christianity, Episcopalians must do two things: 1) get deeply rooted in our neighborhoods and discover the stories, gifts, and wisdom of the communities and cultures around us; and 2) get deeply rooted in the Episcopal Way and discover the stories, gifts, and wisdom of this church."*

In *The Episcopal Way*, we took up that challenge in two ways. First, we examined the major markers for life in the second decade of the twenty-first century—such as social media, multi-tasking, networks, flattened authority, globalization, and secularism—and then identified unique elements of the Episcopal Way that might balance or complement those trends.

---

* Eric Law and Stephanie Spellers, *The Episcopal Way,* vol. 1, Church's Teachings for a Changing World (New York: Church Publishing, 2014), 7.

Then we turned the tables to take an honest look at Episcopal Church life, its light and its shadows. We pointed to the church's capacity for adaptation *and* its fear of change; its love of beauty *and* its sometimes idolatrous relation to liturgical and aesthetic norms; its history of generosity *and* the shadow of elitism; the high value we place on reason *and* the temptation to think ourselves right out of love for God. From there, we listened for wisdom beyond the church, to see what others could teach us about following God on the Episcopal Way.

Four years after launching this project, we found ourselves convinced this conversational method is more urgent now than ever—for the life of the church and the life of our world.

Eric: I wonder . . . what did you like most about our book?

Stephanie: I hope what comes through is our genuine love of the Episcopal Church and the God this church helps both of us to follow. As I look at it, this book feels like a love letter to the church. When you love someone, you accept and celebrate what they are, and you want to be a part of what they're becoming.

It also feels like we were leading people through a dance: looking back to the rich gifts of the past, looking forward to the challenges and promise of the future, looking within at the practices and stories of the Church, looking out to the wisdom and longing of the world. That's the only way Episcopalians can live faithfully—looking, touching and engaging all those realities. It's like the Via Media in action.

Via Media: the "middle way" or a comprehensive, "both/and" path that draws on the wisdom of multiple perspectives to move toward a fuller understanding of the truth.

Eric: I'm glad we addressed the essential question: is the church relevant for people who might say, "I'm spiritual but not religious"? Some people dismiss Christianity because it seems like it's always looking inward, like the church knows all the answers and excludes the rest.

Stephanie: Yes, I think the book really makes a different case: we know some, the world knows some. If you're spiritual but not religious, you just might know things we don't know, and you might appreciate some of the things we've worked out over hundreds of years. Let's walk it out together.

Eric: I also like that we don't protect the church. We challenged the church. You've got to talk about how privileged we have been and still are, as a whole church (in terms of our status as a majority white, majority middle- and upper-middle-class church, with a disproportionate number of college-educated members). Don't hide from that—take responsibility for it.

Stephanie: What about for you, Eric—what part of the story felt most important to you?

Eric: My passion is for the church to continue to learn from the world. When we choose not to do the life-giving thing— not to follow Jesus, do justice, love mercy, walk humbly with God—when we need to be pulled back to the source, sometimes the world helps us to do that. For instance, there are a lot of exciting things happening in science and in the business world. Everybody is talking about relationship.

Stephanie: Yeah, I now have a checking account that's called "Relationship Checking." Come on!

Eric: Some businesses are figuring out how to relate, how to have a social purpose in the world, and how to make money. Putting our faith next to what goes on in the world, we come to a new way that is more faithful than anything we had before.

Stephanie: Speaking of testing things in the real world, it was important that this book (and future volumes) featured things like the "Try This" exercises and "Road Rules" for engaging others and study guides for continuing the conversation. I am reminded of that wonderful Latin phrase: *lex orandi, lex credendi*. It's literally "The law of praying is the law of belief." But it really means, if you want to know what we believe, watch how we pray. Watch what we do. Even as we were writing and teaching in the book, some of that teaching could only happen by asking people to go do something. That's the Episcopal Way. Go have an experience and then we can talk some more. Go talk to someone else and come talk to me. That's where God is waiting.

I almost feel the process was just as important as the topics we addressed in the first book. In other words, social media and the internet or network theory are important, but they're bound to change over generations, cultures, and just time. You have to remember the exercise of drawing the connections, trying it out and reflecting and trying again. That is a core Episcopal practice.

Eric: So we're asking people, "How would you work the process we've named for yourself?" Lift beyond the specific issues. Learn the Episcopal Way of walking faithfully with whatever the world throws at you.

Stephanie: I wonder which part of the story you would change?

Eric: Starting in the 1970s, the Episcopal Church embraced psychology as a field that shaped much of how we do church, how we live in community. It's given us the Myers-Briggs personality inventory and Clinical Pastoral Education in hospitals, both as an almost uniform requirement for ordination. Sometimes we embrace psychology too much. For instance, the priest is expected to be like a one-on-one counselor with people. Now that I think about it, that might be one reason why this church hasn't grown much over the last few decades. It's impossible for a church to grow beyond 150 people if the priest is this professional, personal caretaker for all the people.

Then again, I wish we could listen more to the latest research from intercultural studies. For example, there is a stage-theory called the Developmental Model of Intercultural Sensitivity by Milton J. Bennett:

- In *denial*, we avoid difference.

- In *defense*, we polarize our differences.

- In *minimization*, we minimize our differences and uphold our sameness (where most of us are today).

- We need to move beyond minimization to *acceptance* of difference. That's when we are curious about difference and want to learn more. Look at the song, "In Christ There Is No East or West," then look at the last verse: "In Christ now meet both East and West." That's the next stage in our development.

- Then comes *adaptation*, as we adapt and adjust our behaviors and thinking in different cultural environments, without losing who we are. Do you realize that's basically the Via Media? What we propose as a church is actually an advanced level of intercultural sensitivity development, so it's not surprising that people may really struggle with it. Intercultural theory helps us name where we've been and where we are now and where we hope to be going, and maybe why it's so hard to shift from one to the other.

Stephanie: I notice we devoted a chapter to the need for the church to fall in love with God again. We also had a long list of the church's gifts to the world around us. In both places, we didn't say that much about Jesus. We spoke of story, we spoke of Scripture, we spoke of God, we spoke of ritual and traditions, we spoke of saints. We didn't really name relationship with Jesus as one of the gifts—the primary gift—of the church to the world.

Sometimes we're sensitive to a fault, trying not to offend anybody, so we don't talk about Jesus. Soon after we wrote *The Episcopal Way*, Michael Curry was elected presiding bishop of the Episcopal Church, and he invited us to see ourselves as not just the Church but as the Episcopal branch of the Jesus Movement. I think today, as a church, we are exploring and waking up to the power of Jesus as the center of our lives. We're finding our words and getting comfortable sharing Jesus. His love can heal a changing and often hurting world. He's a force for love, liberation and life, and we don't need to shy away from him at the heart of our life.

Eric: What would you say to someone you're companioning who is in the "next generation" (under the age of thirty) or new to the faith?

Stephanie: When people are newer to faith, they may feel like they can only be learners and listeners. I hope they know they also have something to bring. I hope they know they can bless this venerable old church, as much as it blesses them. I hope they know God rejoices in working in their lives as much as God has been praised in the lives of saints.

I hope they also get encouragement to be curious and humble. We can say, "I am absolutely in love with God as I know him in Jesus, *and* I am absolutely curious about how you experience the divine and come into wholeness, too." We need that kind of curiosity and humility in the world today.

Eric: I agree. I would want them to know that their story is an important part of the conversation. They are part of the sacred. So often we dismiss young people's stories. We say things like, "You call that music? You call texting communicating?" We could really help them to value their own story as they read the Bible. See what this book has to do with the world today. What in their own experience is challenged or affirmed by the story? In fact, we could simply say, "Don't just read the book. Do the book."

Stephanie: Exactly! There's a reason why we shared our own stories early on in the book. It was an invitation to others to put their lives into conversation with the story of God, the church, the world.

Eric: They can navigate through all the polarizing issues of the day—including politics, media, the erosion of trust, personal and moral behavior, sexual harassment and everything else—if they choose to be curious and walk with a diverse community. Please don't do faith in an isolated community or with people who think just like you. That just continues the polarizations. Be with people who are different, people who ask you to re-tell your story because they haven't heard it before. Be with people who tell their stories and help you to discover the greater God story together. That's the Episcopal Way.

Stephanie: In our strongest moments, we understand faith is not about arriving somewhere. It really is about walking the way with companions. And if we didn't say that as clearly in the first book, we're saying it now.

Chapter 2

A Conversation on History with Thomas Ferguson

"Christians have always adapted, always been diverse, and always needed to embrace global realities. Anglicanism, from the Reformation to the birth of the Episcopal Church, to the development of the Anglican Communion, has done the same. We can only hope to be as faithful as our forebears, as we are all cocreators of the Christianity that is coming into being." *

Tom Ferguson is a scholar (faculty at Bexley-Seabury Institute in Chicago), priest (rector of St. John's Episcopal Church in Sandwich, Massachusetts) and blogger (crustyolddean.blogspot.com). His volume on history—*The Episcopal Story: Birth and Rebirth*—required all those gifts. Tom introduced not only the nearly 250-year-old story of the Episcopal Church but the sweep of Christian history from the birth of the faith through its initial spread, into the rise of Christendom, the Middle Ages, the Reformation, Anglicanism's birth in England and

---

* Thomas C. Ferguson, *The Episcopal Story: Birth and Rebirth,* vol. 2, Church's Teachings for a Changing World (New York: Church Publishing, 2015), 98.

America, nineteenth-century mission, and the contemporary Episcopal Church and Anglican Communion.

Stephanie: *I wonder . . . as you review The Episcopal Story, what do you like best?*

Tom: Looking back over the book, I've come to appreciate the introduction more and more. Sometimes introductions can look hopelessly dated, because what the author has written doesn't age well. I decided to organize the book around the themes of diversity, adaptation, and globalization in part out of necessity: trying to boil 2,000 years of Christian history into 100 pages means you can't get lost in weeds. You have to think about the lenses through which you view the past.

I think the key themes of diversity, adaptation, and globalization have become, if anything, even more relevant since the book came out. Christianity is always in a process of change and adaptation, and it's becoming increasingly clear to me we are in the midst of a massive change and shift in how we do church. We have been since the middle of the twentieth century. Realizing that we are doing what Christians have done again and again, what Christians have done anew in each generation, should give us some comfort in the midst of our challenges. Our forebears navigated diversity, adaptation, globalization. We are doing it. Our descendants will, too.

Stephanie: *That's so very true. Are there also parts of the book that feel even more important to you now?*

Tom: I'm probably overly fond of the chapters on the history of the early church—and not just because my PhD focus was in Early Christianity and this is where I like to geek out. In both academic and parish teaching and formation, I've found a lot of folks don't have a lot of interest in the early church. They wonder what relevance it has in our context. The very "otherness" of that context can be off-putting. So yes, we don't believe in witches and that God divinely appoints emperors. Yet there are startling similarities, as well, that I think we overlook at our peril and can learn from.

The Christianity of the first centuries unfolded in a diverse, globalized, rapidly changing world that was at times aggressive and hostile to the Christian message. Looking at how Christianity adapted to that context can teach us about our own reality.

Stephanie: Speaking of change . . . if you could add another chapter or two, perhaps to speak to this very moment, what would you change now about the book?

Tom: I would have liked to have had more focus on the church in the twentieth and twenty-first centuries—even though I realize writing a book is like a game of Jenga, and to start changing pieces in one section would cascade throughout the whole project. Yet I think the period from 1910 to 1960 is an extraordinarily important one for the Episcopal Church: it's where a lot of our modern structure starts to emerge (for example the Church Pension Fund; the Executive Council; the presiding bishop becoming a full-time job; diocesan structures becoming more active; continuing engagement in global mission with growing awareness of its complexities; the emerging Civil Rights movement and questions of racial and cultural diversity).

"There's a dizzying diversity in what it means to be a follower of Jesus. Study of the church's history helps to reinforce this."

Since we still have a number of people with us who lived through our modern history, I think many Episcopalians have a better grasp of what happened in the 1960s than the 1910s. But that period from 1910 to 1960 is crucial in shaping the latter twentieth-century Episcopal Church.

Stephanie: Finally, imagine you're a companion to a young person or someone who is fairly new to the faith. What would you highlight for them in your book?

Tom: I say time and again in the book that we're always going through processes of change and adaptation. This is, frankly, still news to lots of people, many of whom seem to think the church changes slowly, or never, and that the way the church currently looks is the way it's always been. When I was a campus chaplain, I engaged a lot of young adults who had extraordinarily negative associations with Christianity. I would highlight to them, as I would to anyone new to the church, not to let anybody tell you with confidence what church "is." Being a person of faith isn't any one thing; there's a dizzying diversity in what it means to be a follower of Jesus, and study of the church's history helps to reinforce this. Experience it for yourself, while drawing from the deep reservoir of our past.

Chapter 3

A Conversation on Theology with Jesse Zink

"The ancient faith Episcopalians inherit is linked with the future church emerging in our midst. Our theological heritage is not something to be confined to a dusty back room; it is to be put at the center of our life together, where these ancient ideas continue to be relevant to our work for a future church."*

Jesse Zink serves now as the principal of Montreal Diocesan Theological College in Canada, where he continues to take the ancient faith off the shelf and brush off the dust. Or, as he put it in *A Faith for the Future*: "I want … to share the Good News of Jesus Christ and to help others discover more fully how The Episcopal Church understands it."

Zink encouraged readers to craft a summary of that Good News for themselves. Then he shared his own: "You are loved with a love unlike any else that leads to a life unlike any else—now go, show that love & life to others. #grace #gospel" (134

---

* Jesse Zink, *A Faith for the Future,* vol. 3, Church Teachings for A Changing World (New York: Church Publishing, 2016), vi.

characters, which made an excellent tweet before Twitter bumped the limit to 280).

He shaped the book around a different, even more essential theological statement claimed by Christians the world over: the Nicene Creed. He proceeded to treat the various theological elements present in the creed—God, Creation, Humanity and Sin, Jesus of Nazareth, Jesus the Christ, the Holy Spirit and the Trinity, Baptism, Church, Eucharist, Mission, and Eschatology.

Stephanie: What part of the story or the book did you like best?

Jesse: Writing this book helped me to clarify so much of my thinking. There's a clear connection between what we do in church and what we do outside of church. I tried to structure the book around the Nicene Creed, baptism, and Eucharist—things that traditionally happen inside a church building, that also give us an orientation for living in the world.

I find it obnoxious that people say Episcopalians don't "do" theology. The more time I spend with the 1979 Book of Common Prayer, the more I realize what a theologically rich resource it is. You could spend all day on the primacy of Eucharist and baptism and the relation between the two. You could spend all day thinking and more importantly living this stuff.

Baptism, for instance, is a reminder of how we've died to our sin and risen to new life in Christ. It challenges some of the achievement-oriented, task-oriented nature of the world we live in, certainly the world I live in. There's all this pressure to do everything right, for children, for parents, for co-workers. The message of baptism is, "We're imperfect people, but we're orienting ourselves by God's grace, re-orienting to live a life that Christ lived, the life expressed in the Baptismal Covenant."

In Eucharist, we realize the kind of life that God wants for us. A life in which we are at one with God in confession. At one with one another in passing the Peace. A life where we're constantly seeking to expand our Eucharistic community, to draw more people into that life of thanksgiving. True, we put all this emphasis on worship, but the story of our worship doesn't end when service ends on Sunday. Part of the great joy and challenge of being Episcopalian is taking that orientation and way of life so it orients our lives in the world as well.

Stephanie: *And what seems especially important to you, as you look at the story you shared?*

Jesse: I was trying to frame the book with a practice: Look at the world around you. Most likely, it's an increasingly secular world. Fewer people are going to church—fewer to The Episcopal Church or to church in general—but this is a world where a lot of religious activity happens. We speak of belief, which is a way of saying trust. Where do you put your trust in this day and age? A lot of people put their trust in money, trust in power (especially power over someone else), trust in a particular identity. You might not think you have religious commitments, but look around. Where do you put your trust? Those are religious things. My question is: Do those things lead to abundant life?

Sometimes people think, "If you're a religious or Christian person, you're doing a funny and counter-cultural thing. You don't fit in secular society." In fact, you do. There's no shortage of religion out there, and not just world religions. What we need to do as Episcopalians is spend a little time in theological reflection about how the commitments we make in our prayers and creeds lead to life that is truly abundant, that has something to say to the world.

Stephanie: *What part of the book and the story would you change? We all turn in a manuscript and then think, "Oh, let me just add this!"*

Jesse: I spent a couple of chapters on Jesus. I found it helpful to think about the story of the road to Emmaus, the day Jesus rises from the dead. His followers are walking the road to Emmaus, and they meet a stranger, tell the stranger about their pain, how they hoped this one would redeem Israel, but then he was killed. And now they're so afraid, they're running from Jerusalem. But even in their fear they invite the stranger to have a meal with them, and their hearts are strangely warmed when he breaks the bread. That night, they're turned around and they go back to Jerusalem.

For me, that's an example of how we get turned around with Jesus. There's a lot of pain and hurt out there. If we think about it, we all have places that are like Jerusalem to us—a place of pain, fear, anxiety—and we've got to get out of there. We may not fear for our lives (some do), but we all have brokenness and pain in some part of our lives. Meeting Jesus on the road, meeting Jesus in broken bread, turns us around and helps us to see pain in a new way. It transforms our brokenness and leads us to new life.

A word Christians use for this complex journey is reconciliation. It's not easy. It takes a lot of work to go back to the places I'm afraid to go back to. Then I meet Jesus in prayer and in Eucharist, I meet Jesus in other people, meet Jesus in the Bible. Little by little, I feel the push of the Spirit to go back and see those places of pain in a new way. You don't get there immediately. It's about the orientation for our life. Orientation in Christ gives me courage, heals my brokenness,

eschatology: from the Greek "last" (ἔσχατος) and "study" (-λογία); the study of "end things," whether the end of a life, the end of the age, the end of the world or the Kingdom of God.

leads a step closer to reconciliation. That message is even more profound and relevant today.

Another point I'd take further is eschatology. That's the end or the final consummation of all things in the Bible. It's an area of theology that Episcopalians and others have neglected in recent decades. I get that; biblical books like Revelation stretch our credulity furthest. People use words like apocalypse, and everybody thinks more about zombies than Jesus. What I like about eschatology is that it really is written for people who live in fear, turmoil and oppression. Eschatology is their hope for the future. How do you live eschatologically, hope-fully, especially when there doesn't seem to be a lot of hope?

For instance, I've been reading a lot of William Stringfellow, an Episcopal layman and lawyer and theologian during the Civil Rights Movement. He wrote *An Ethic for Aliens in a Strange Land*, where he says the core gospel message sounds like individual conversion, but has structural implications, as well. It's deeply political. That's what we need to hear. When your theology is like Stringfellow's, and it's deeply grounded in eschatology, you see how structures in the world need to change to be more in line with the vision God has for the world.

I just gave a talk at the American Academy of Religion's annual gathering in November, and it was on Anglicanism and migration. One point I made: migrants are people on a journey. What do they need? Strength for the journey and a sense of where they're going. That's true for Syrians in Greece, the Rohingya in Malaysia, Iraqis in America—they all need strength and sustenance, and to see where they're going. It can't be a refugee camp forever.

If Christians are like migrants, then we too need strength for the journey and a sense of where we're going. We're not so good at saying, "This is our vision for the kind of society we hope for, the Kingdom of God." We need to provide some texture and content for that. What does it look like to have restored and renewed relationship between people and people, people and creation, people and God?

Part of being a minister of the gospel and a theologian is to point out eschatological moments when they happen. Look! Did you see that moment of reconciliation? That's what we're looking for. You might only see it in a flash, but point to it. Hold it up, as a clue to where we're headed. Our Presiding Bishop Michael Curry talks about turning the world from the nightmare it so often is into the dream of God. What does it look like? Have you ever seen it? Point it out to me.

There's something really important there. Can we be people of hope and wonder in an age of fear and anxiety and loathing? Can we listen again to the final verse of "It Came Upon a Midnight Clear" and really hear it?

Yet with the woes of sin and strife
The world hath suffered long;

Beneath the angel-strain have rolled
Two thousand years of wrong;
And man, at war with man, hears not
The love song which they bring:
O hush the noise, ye men of strife,
And hear the angels sing.

That verse is totally eschatological. It moves me to tears.

Stephanie: I hear your message and I feel it, too. As we wrap up, what would you especially share with a person who is under age thirty or new to the faith, if you were their companion?

Jesse: I would invite them to see the world with religious eyes. And to ask that question: are you finding abundant life in the things you put your trust in? Can you see a long-term future in those things? Is it a sustainable life? I find that abundant life in the God who is made known in Jesus. I do that not because I have to, not because my parents told me to, not because it's some old, fuddy-duddy tradition, but because I genuinely find more of life in it. Oh sure, I've got my own idols who distract me from God. But somehow, in trying to put Jesus in the center of my life, in prayer and in worship and in disciplines, I do find something I can't find anywhere else.

I've been reading this book by James A. K. Smith: *You Are What You Love: The Spiritual Power of Habit.* We are not people who are rational. We are motivated by our desires. They take us in a direction we don't want sometimes. But worship trains our desires. Repetition of this act, that ritual—it helps to train our desires in a God-ward direction. That's so good and so necessary. If you want to know us, come pray with us. Don't just do it once—keep doing it. I find that such a rich way of reflecting on faith and belief.

Chapter 4

A Conversation on Social Witness with Winnie Varghese

"It is the work of our salvation to seek justice and serve one another. The work of liturgy, study, prayer, and conversation in our congregations effects a transformation of our personal lives toward an ever-increasing recognition of the humanity of others and the sacredness of creation."*

"The Episcopal witness in the world is particular to a place and time. . . . [W]e trust that God has made us to bear light in this broken world."**

In writing *Church Meets World*, Winnie Varghese accepted a challenge a lot like pinning down mercury: summarize the biblical, theological and historical principles and figures who have guided Episcopal social justice. Then explore contemporary social challenges like creation care, racism, sexuality and relationships, gender identity, economic justice, and war. And

---

* Winnie Varghese, *Church Meets World,* vol. 4, Church's Teachings for a Changing World (New York: Church Publishing, 2016), 5.

** Varghese, 6.

don't forget to explain concepts like "power," "social location," and "intersectionality"—all in less than 100 pages.

Winnie serves as the Director of Justice and Reconciliation at Trinity Episcopal Church Wall Street in New York City. She spoke to Eric about how she approaches the book and the whole concept of Christian social witness now, given the issues emerging in our time.

Eric: I wonder which part of the book do you like best?

Winnie: I find our history, for good and for bad, both inspiring and challenging. Some prominent figures in our history have been greatly admired in one area, but they were not so great on other issues or in their personal lives. This may be how we think about the saints, too. Their stories are important to Christian life—their whole story, the failures as well as the brilliance. We can imagine our own lives in the same way. We seek justice, but no one will do it perfectly. Still, we persevere. I need to hear that.

Eric: I wonder which part of the book is the most important to you?

social location: a lens for noticing and being honest about all the parts of our identity—our national origin, class, race, gender expression, and other factors

Winnie: It was important for me to introduce the language of social location, power, and other terms that I hope would be used by the Episcopal Church when we talk about this work.

I think we use a lot of theological terms like incarnation and reconciliation, but we are less consistent in using a common language on power and identity. It felt important to introduce these terms, for us to be part of the wider conversation with others who seek justice.

Eric: And which part of the story would you change, knowing what you do now?

Winnie: I was worrying that the book was heavily focused on criminal justice. However, in the past year, it was clearly the issue of the day for anyone looking at racism and how it informs our whole social system. In that, I feel validated.

There is something profoundly sinful about the way we are living now, and we have defaulted to old patterns as if they are normal. I could not have imagined when I was writing this book that we would be once again thinking about full-on nuclear war, this time with North Korea. I would have written a whole different book.

Since the presidential election, gender discrimination and sexual harassment have come to the forefront, and so many public figures have been taken down. Women and men have always been harassed and abused, but we're reckoning with it. I could not imagine this moment. Addressing this issue in the workplace and politics—the whole #metoo movement—would need to be a large section. It's simply that important.

In light of this issue, I have to be honest. I used a quote from a very prominent figure in the Episcopal Church that I wish now I hadn't. I knew there were lawsuits and rumors of sexual harassment surrounding this person. There were people who were required to be quiet. It was also part of the church culture that harassed people were not willing to go public. That's the thing about sexual harassment. People know the truth, they know they're participating in an oppressive system that runs counter to the gospel, and no one can say anything. When I was working on the book, I thought he was a brilliant writer and I decided it was okay to use the quote. Given where we are now, where his personal behavior is recognized as a real justice issue, I think it was a mistake and I would have found some other equally good quote. I feel differently aware, but I don't know how you fix it.

Eric: You raise a good question. Does the revelation of sexual harassment discredit everything that a person has done?

Winnie: I wonder if there is a way to frame a citation and quote from such a person that is just. It might begin with, "We are living in a time where we are holding people accountable for what they say and write and for their personal behavior."

Eric: I facilitate the Anti-Racism Training at Sewanee School of Theology every year. Participants read an article from the Sewanee Theological Review that chronicles the history of integration at the School of Theology in the 1950s. In the article, a few of the bishops then were quoted saying what we would consider horrific things about race. The students were shocked to read the quotes from bishops who were revered in their dioceses. I said to them, "Now you know. What are you going to do about this?"

Winnie: That's one important way forward.

Eric: I wonder what you would focus on if you were a companion walking with the "next" generation?

Winnie: Having been a college chaplain for ten years, I would invite new Episcopalians into the practices of the church, however they are manifested in their contexts. A primary piece of our identity is that we participate together. There's so much more to faith than belief and comprehension. I would offer a lot of hospitality. It is important for us to be generous, inviting fully and appropriately for those seeking. I would invite people to be mindful of the practice of seeking God around us. The way to do that, we know from Jesus, is to listen for people whose suffering we see and recognize him.

> The king will say to those at his right hand, "Come, you that are blessed by my Father, inherit the kingdom prepared for you from the foundation of the world; for I was hungry and you gave me food, I was thirsty and you gave me something to drink, I was a stranger and you welcomed me, I was naked and you gave me clothing, I was sick and you took care of me, I was in prison and you visited me." Then the righteous will answer him, "Lord, when was it that we saw you . . .?" And the king will answer them, "Truly I tell you, just as you did it to one of the least of these who are members of my family, you did it to me." (Matthew 25: 34–37a, 40)

If we follow this path, we find ourselves where we are supposed to be. Our tradition invites us to live fully in the world around us, to look and be and see God in the world. We don't think the sacred and the holy is only within our religious practice. Our practice drives us out into the world so we understand it differently and eventually take part in transforming it.

Chapter 5

A Conversation on Ethics with Scott Bader-Saye

"The Episcopal ethos is a pattern of living shaped by the practices of prayer and holiness, the belief in creation and Incarnation, and the authorities of Scripture, tradition, and reason. This is not a comprehensive list, but it gives us a constellation of identity markers that provide some idea of where to start when we ask what it means to live well as a human being from the perspective of the Episcopal tradition."*

In *Formed by Love*, Scott Bader-Saye provides an Episcopal road map for living a moral and ethical life. He begins by defining the Episcopal way of doing ethics in the context of our fast-changing world. Then he shifts to explore big questions like . . .

- How to be happy and good
- How to do what you want
- How not to follow the rules

---

* Scott Bader-Saye, *Formed by Love,* vol. 4, Church's Teachings for a Changing World (New York: Church Publishing, 2017), 15.

- How to love like Jesus
- How to keep justice just
- How to find the good in others

That flows into a conversation about how to be moral and ethical in our prayers, our work, our eating, and our play. He still guides seminarians through those big life questions as an ethics professor at the Episcopal Seminary of the Southwest in Austin, Texas.

Eric: What part of the book do you like best?

Scott: I like the early chapters where I tried to help people to redefine what they think of as "ethics": away from a set of limiting rules, and toward a more aspirational vision of what ethics is. Rules and punishment are fundamentally limiting. I want to give people a different vision of how we move toward blessings. Reflection on ethics helps us know how to live well for the sake of self and others.

Eric: That's what appealed most to you. What part of the book is the most important to you?

Scott: The last chapter on fear and Compline (the prayer we offer late at night, before bed) seems to be the most important chapter of the book, because it speaks to the temptation to be manipulated or paralyzed by fear. When you pray Compline while paying attention to fear, you realize how much of Compline is really about helping us to trust that God is our security.

ethics: more than a set of limiting rules, Episcopal ethics seeks the way to live well for the sake of self and others.

We don't do that in a naïve sense. It's not a fairy tale promise that everything is going to be great, but a promise that our ultimate security, the things that are good in the world, are secured by God. They don't have to be secured by violence or by attacking the stranger or fearing those around us. Being able to connect Compline, a particular Episcopal resource, to something that's pressing in the world around us was really important.

The chapter titled "How to Find Good in Others" dovetails with the chapter on Compline. Both of these chapters speak to crucial cultural issues at the moment. The chapter on finding good in others helps us see how we can expect to find goodness outside of our own religious tradition. Here is the challenge: if you want to say our religion helps us to be better people, then does that imply that people who are not Christians or who are not Episcopalians, can't be good in the same way? That's not the Episcopal way of seeing the world. Our doctrine of creation helps us to expect that we're going to find goodness scattered through the world, regardless of whether people are followers of Jesus or not.

But then, are we implying that being good or not is totally unrelated to your practice of faith? That's not the Episcopal Way either. In that chapter, I was trying to help people to affirm that the resources of our faith and our relationship with God, Christ and the Spirit, all those help us to see what is good and act on it. It doesn't have to be an exclusive vision of where we're going to find goodness. The doctrine of creation ought to open us up to expect goodness from lots of unexpected places.

I was hoping to help people to clear some space to be ready to find goodness in people they disagree with, people who are different from them, people who might scare them, and not assume in advance that any one group has cornered the market on being ethical or being moral or being good.

Eric: *Would you say that's particularly Episcopal?*

Scott: Yes, absolutely. Most of the Protestant traditions tended to be shaped by a stronger notion of how original sin has impacted us. I don't mean that Episcopalians ignore original sin. But the way many traditions talk, whether it is filtered through Martin Luther or John Calvin, sin has such a disrupting and disorienting effect that it is hard to see how goodness can still emerge prior to having been redeemed. It's hard to imagine that anyone who is not already a Christian can be good, when you can't expect to find any goodness in the world around you. One thing the Episcopal Church had held onto from the Catholic tradition was a stronger notion of the ongoing presence of goodness in creation. Sin has not entirely defaced the goodness that God has made.

I grew up Presbyterian. Sometimes, in the Reformed tradition, we elevated the sovereignty of God by denigrating humanity. The worse we are, the better God must be. So beating ourselves up became an important part of talking about how amazing God is—after all, we are so awful, and God still loves and saves us. This is a kind of perverse zero-sum game. That God can only be great because we are so terrible.

As I moved into the Episcopal Church, I recognized that there is a different assumption: the greater God is, the greater is that which God made. Elevating God's majesty and sovereignty can go hand-in-hand with elevating our picture of humanity. If

God made us, God made us good in the way that totally reflects who God is. Yes, we are sinful. We are fallen. But there is a potential for more.

Eric: I wonder: is there any part of the book you would change, especially given where our society is now?

Scott: The book came out fairly recently, and I even got a Donald Trump quote before he was elected president. It was clear that he was a cultural force who was reshaping our conversation. Even before he took office, the world was becoming the kind of place we are seeing now. Our cultural conversations were breaking down with greater polarization. I started the book by talking about the challenges of being polarized as a culture and as a society. I talked about the struggle with the sense of identity, and how many people react to these challenges with outrage. This description of our cultural context is still alive.

Eric: What more would you say, if you had room?

Scott: I've been doing some reading in moral psychology—Jonathan Haidt's *The Righteous Mind*, Joshua Greene's *Moral Tribes*, and Daniel Kaheman's *Thinking Fast and Slow*. Over the last five to ten years, these psychologists have consistently told us most of our moral judgment rises not out of reflection but intuition. People rarely make ethical decisions based on reason. It's a reaction out of intuition, out of their gut.

Haidt said our reasoning is always a *post-hoc* (after the fact) justification of where our gut is taking us. Some moral psychologists and philosophers are pushing back, saying our reasoning is not always merely self-justifying. What's becoming clear to me is, the pattern they described seems to ring true as I look around at moral conversation and moral actions—even when I examine myself. This might be the reason why people who read our books don't necessarily change their behavior. Our gut response needs to change.

Brian Stevenson, who wrote *Just Mercy*, talks a lot about the importance of proximity. The way forward may not be about using words and trying to reason our way to this or that conclusion. The best way forward for change and choosing well and living well may have to do with finding ways to come into proximity with those we might find different or even scary. I don't think we should stop thinking and reasoning together. But I don't think just reasoning together is going to make a difference if we are not moving into proximity with the people we're talking about.

Left-leaning Christians need to connect with right-leaning Christians and say, "Let me hear your story" and vice versa. How do we come into proximity with each other without the posture of judgment or superiority? How do we express actual curiosity and that we're not there to study them as strange creatures who voted for the other person? I think the key is, as Jonathan Haidt points out at the end of his book, you don't start by talking about difficult topics where you disagree. You come into proximity to share a fellowship or a meal. Only later you talk about the difficult topic. You have to discover a common humanity first. Creating spaces where we can do that is essential. It sounds kind of simple, but we don't do it that much.

Eric: I hear you. As we close, I wonder . . . what would you highlight about ethics if you were a companion walking with a younger person or someone who is new to faith?

Scott: I would emphasize the idea that we are called to find the balance between form and freedom. I would say to the next generations that the Episcopal way gives form to our lives, which is something we need in the midst of a culture that feels pretty formless and chaotic. But within that form, there is room for freedom. There is room for improvisation. In fact, freedom and improvisation are invited as a natural outgrowth of the form that's given to us in the Episcopal pattern of following Jesus.

I would say ours is not the sort of Christianity they might see in news stories, where the Christian groups you see are the loudest or angriest or the most contentious. We are inviting you into a way of faith that is not primarily defined by who we are against, but defined by a path that has form, and then opens onto a freedom that allows us to engage others, to engage new ideas, to explore new possibilities and to open our eyes to witness life and blessing. There is a way of entering into the Christian tradition that doesn't mean closing ourselves off from the other people and other aspects of the world.

This allows us to have a deeper appreciation of the good we may have already intimated in our own lives and experiences. All of us have places in our lives that need to revise and reform. That's real, and we don't need to hide that. But we don't start with things you need to repudiate, because that work is not really going to bear fruit.

I have said that ethics is aspirational: we start with what we aspire to, and that invigorates our desire. So much of what I see in younger generations as the work of ethics or moral statement comes in the form of protest, resistance, and outrage. This is good, but it can burn you out if it's your only mode of moral expression. These moral expressions have to be situated within a vision of what is the good that we are moving toward, what is lovely and desirable and beautiful that we aspire to. This aspiration will ultimately keep us going.

Chapter 6

A Conversation on Ministry with Michael Curry

"When we use the phrase the "Jesus Movement," we're actually pointing back to the earliest days of Jesus's teaching and his followers moving in his revolutionary footsteps in the power of the Spirit. Together with them, we're following Jesus and growing loving, liberating, life-giving relationship with God, with each other, and with creation." *

It's not too much to say the book *Following the Way of Jesus* is itself a multi-partner conversation about Episcopal ministry in light of the Jesus Movement. The core of the book is three chapters by Michael Curry, presiding bishop of the Episcopal Church. In them, he summarizes the biblical and historic underpinnings for understanding the church as the Jesus Movement. Then he helps us to stay centered on the sacrificial, unselfish, life-giving love of Jesus. Eventually, he paints the vision of God's dream of justice, healing, and freedom for all people and all of creation.

---

* Michael B. Curry, et. al., *Following the Way of Jesus,* vol. 6, Church's Teachings for a Changing World (New York: Church Publishing, 2017), 2.

Six ministry leaders and thinkers then take Curry's writings and use them as a jumping-off point for reflection:

- Megan Castellan focuses on reclaiming the ministry of evangelism and spreading the Good News of Jesus, who loves and heals and sets all of us free.

- Anthony Guillén brings multiple perspectives and voices together in his reflection on launching new ministries with Latino, black, Asiamerican and indigenous communities.

- Kellan Day offers insight on young adult ministry, where she finds authenticity and true faith are the things that matter most.

- Broderick Greer proves that no one can pursue racial reconciliation without also committing to racial justice and truth-telling.

- Nora Gallagher imagines ministry that truly honors the kingdom of God right here on the earth.

- Robert Wright introduces adaptive leadership, or how to turn institutions and people in new directions and truly lead a movement.

Eric: What part of the book or story do you like best or find the most important?

Michael: Following the way of Jesus is intrinsically counter-cultural to every culture and frankly to every personality. I think that came through consistently in every chapter. I'll be honest: in many respects, the Christian brand has been hijacked by a brand of Christianity that does not reflect the face of Jesus of Nazareth, which *is* the way of sacrificial, cross-shaped love.

Jesus simply didn't sacrifice his life to get something out of it, and that's what love is supposed to look like. This is nothing new for Christians. Dietrich Bonhoeffer said it, Martin Luther King Jr. said it, so many have said it. But it's not at the heart of what we hear from many brands of Christianity today.

I'm not judging anyone as I say this. I guess I'm preaching to myself, because the way of Jesus is counter to my *own* way. I'm human, so I'm inclined to see everything as peripheral to Michael being at the center. So Christianity is really calling for the new Copernican Revolution. You know: Copernicus discovered the world revolves around the sun, not the other way around. For most of us, the revolution is living as if there's something outside of ourselves that really is the center of the universe. It has personal, social consequences.

I would submit that the love of Jesus, really following Jesus, could be the focus of a new reformation. The sixteenth-century reformers had to reclaim faith. It may be in our time we have to reclaim the way of love. Look at the conversation between Jesus and the young lawyer. What does it take to obtain eternal life? In the Gospel of Mark's version (10:17–31), the lawyer says, "Moses said love God and love your neighbor." Jesus said, "That's right! Now you're close to the kingdom." The Gospel of Luke has a similar conversation in chapter 18; Jesus also tells the parable of the Good Samaritan (chapter 10). Who is the neighbor? The one who showed mercy. Go and do likewise. Go and live.

But when the Gospel of John speaks of such things, he goes off-script. Jesus has the audacity to add to the Ten Commandments and gives them a new commandment: love one another, as I've loved you (John 13:34). It's stunning. Returning to his

Jesus Movement: the ongoing community of people who center their lives on Jesus and follow him into loving, liberating, life-giving relationships with God, each other, and creation

unselfish, sacrificial way of love may be a new reformation of Christianity.

That message is profoundly suited for a time like ours. We live in a world where we can't pretend that other people who are profoundly different from us don't exist. How can you navigate in a world where there are so many different ways of living and believing? I would submit that love is the way that guides us. Not sentimental love, but sacrificial love, following in the way of Jesus. Being open to other people and their experiences as real possibilities for the human family. I suspect that's a unique experience of ours in our time.

Martin Luther King's words haunt me with hope. "We shall either learn to live together as brothers and sisters or perish together as fools." The only way I know to live together as brothers and sisters is the way of love. Given our capacity for self-destruction, we've got to find a better way. The way of narrowness, unbridled nationalism, desecration of the creation—it will not work anymore. The heart of sin is utter selfishness, and that is at the core of all that we suffer. Hear me now: something is at stake. The reality of sin can destroy the earth. That's how dangerous it is. Love is the only way to transform that selfishness into selflessness.

Sometimes people ask, "What's the opposite of love?" Ten years ago, I would have said hate. Now, I see that the opposite of love is selfishness. Jesus got it right: "If any want to become my followers, let them deny themselves and take up their cross daily and follow me. For those who want to save their life will lose it, and those who lose their life for my sake will save it.

What does it profit them if they gain the whole world, but lose or forfeit themselves?" (Luke 9:23–25).

Stephanie: *That really is one of the great challenges for our time, and it's quite present in your book. What would you change or add, if you could go back?*

Michael: We've said the Jesus Movement is following Jesus into loving, liberating, life-giving relationship with God, each other, creation. I would go back and claim following the way of Jesus even more strongly. Asking him to become the center of my life and existence, and having that be the starting place for all our ministries. Of course, that's what he was getting at when he spoke of "following." In light of what I'm beginning to see as the power of sin and selfishness over my life or anybody else's, the only way I can imagine to replace myself at the center, is to put something better and greater at the center. To place Christ at the center of Michael Curry, Christ at the center of the church. A displacement has to happen in order for there to be that replacement.

When Christ is at the center, I get real. It's the fake Michael that thinks it's all about him. That Michael gets lost. To allow Jesus to become the center of my life, to have his way of love also be my way—that can liberate us for life, real life.

Now the replacement of the unbridled self as the center of life, that actually helps me to discover the real me. Imagine the Congress of the United States functioning on the basis of unselfish, sacrificial love. Or for that matter, imagine the General Convention of the Episcopal Church functioning that way. You'd have a different Congress, a different church, a different world.

You do that, and it's a game changer. Youth ministry changes. Creation care changes. Reconciliation changes. Evangelism changes. This isn't anything new; it's ancient stuff. Francis of Assisi and Clare figured this out. I really do believe this may be part of a reformation of our faith in this time, to reclaim this way of being Christian, to follow where Jesus has already led the way.

Eric: So much of what you say applies to all people of faith—really, to all people. Is there anything you would especially want to highlight, if you were walking with someone who is under age thirty or new to the faith?

Michael: I would say to them, let's start with specifics. Bring it from the global to the local. Jesus was trying to show us a way of moving our selfish selves out of the center, and allowing him and his way of sacrificial love to be the center. What would that look like in your life? How would you imagine that? Let's play with that. Then let's apply the same question to other spheres: what if self-giving love guided government, social life, church, personal life? What would we do about sexual harassment? Nuclear powers? Let yourself imagine it.

I suppose it sounds like something very individualistic, but it isn't. We're talking on Christmas Eve, and I keep hearing the song, "Let there be peace on earth and let it begin with me." Start the process of transformation with me. Then I can take my part in the process as it unfolds in the workplace, in social and political contexts.

I would talk with a young person, not just about major ministries but about my own journey. We've been doing this culture work on the church-wide staff. One thing they've helped us to do, is to imagine the workplace culture you'd love to work in. What are the characteristics? What is the current reality, with all its pain? What are the practical steps to get from here to there? Christian ethics speak of moving from what is to what ought to be, and then they ask, "How do you walk there?" Then you say, "What can I do in my own life? Imagine if selfishness was not ruling, but selflessness. What can I do to move us to that vision?"

Jesus was teaching us to do it. How do I live the Lord's Prayer? "Thy kingdom come, thy will be done, on earth as it is in heaven"? That's the conversation we could have, and you could have it with a young person or an old person. All of us have share in this work.

Chapter 7

A Conversation on Scripture with Lauren Winner

"I hope that reading *A Word to Live By* will . . . quicken your curiosity about the Bible, and help you love the Bible more dearly. A suggestion, then: read this book with a Bible nearby—on your computer or (my old-fashioned preference) leaves open on the sofa beside you. Reading about topics in Christian spiritual life—prayer, worship, friendship, Bible study—can take us deeply into the thing, but undertaking what we're reading about will carry us even further." *

Lauren Winner is a popular author and faculty member at Duke Divinity School in Durham, North Carolina. Her love for the Bible shines through the pages of *A Word to Live By*. She knows lots of people feel intimidated by the size of the Bible and the reams of scholarship and opinion surrounding it. So she takes an almost sherpa-like approach to introducing the Bible, guiding readers through its several translations and versions; the shape of the Old Testament and the New Testament (and what

---

* Lauren Winner, *A Word to Live By,* vol. 7, Church's Teachings for a Changing World (New York: Church Publishing, 2017), vii.

those titles even mean); the genres and styles that make up the whole of the Bible (histories, genealogies, gospels, letters, and even an apocalypse or two). She also dwells for a while on the role of Scripture in Episcopal life and prayer—it is, after all, one of the three legs of the stool on which our faith is founded.

Stephanie: I wonder . . . which parts of the book do you like best?

Lauren: In Chapter 2, I mention the spiritual practice of regularly jotting down a summary of the Bible, or of a particular biblical book. This practice probably shows more about the person summarizing than it does about the Bible—about what's important to the person at the moment she makes the summary—so it's a spiritual practice that can connect you to the words of God, and also more deeply acquaint you with yourself and your own current priorities. Then, I offer my own current summary of Scripture.

In that summary, I really do quite like the concept—which is hard for me to get my head around sometimes—that God heals the world of its damage not by grand fiat from on high, not by waving a magic wand at once over all creation, but by working through particular local circumstances to heal all the cosmos. So for example, God works through Israel, and God works through Mary. I don't know why God chooses to go about redemption this way, and the Bible doesn't seem very interested in explaining why. The Bible just shows, over and over, that this is God's preferred mode of fixing broken things.

I also like the notion that Scripture can be read as a series of invitations that God offers us. And finally, I still resonate with the message about Old Testament laws—that is, that although Christians don't follow many of the Old Testament laws (the dietary codes, for example), we can ask what kind of reputation a community that followed such laws might have, and then ask how we, in a given Christian community, could cultivate such a reputation. Maybe a community that followed the law not to boil a goat kid in its mother's milk would have a reputation as a compassionate community, a community that recognized in some way that our life horribly requires the death of other creatures. Maybe a community that followed the Old Testament laws governing how to treat strangers would be known as a community that practiced insane, risky hospitality. What could my local church do to develop a reputation for compassion and hospitality?

Stephanie: *That's a great question for a congregation to sit with. I also wonder which part of the story now feels the most important to you?*

Lauren: There's a difference between writing "an introduction to the Bible" and writing "an introduction to the Bible for Episcopalians." I knew this book needed to be the second, but I thought I might die of boredom (and so would any potential readers) if I attempted to sketch an "Anglican hermeneutics"— that is, if I teased out what distinctive things Anglican greats like Thomas Cranmer and Richard Hooker said about reading the Bible.

It was my colleague Ellen Davis, who teaches Old Testament at Duke Divinity School and who is an Episcopalian herself, who helped me see that the way to go at the "Episcopalianness" of the topic was through the Book of Common Prayer—in other words, what's distinctive about how Episcopalians engage Scripture? In large part, we engage with Scripture in the context of our worship lives, guided by the Prayer Book. Almost half of *A Word to Live By* is devoted to probing that idea from various angles.

Inside that large category—how Episcopalians engage the Bible as part of worship, in concert with and guided by the Prayer Book—what interests me the most is the sheer fact that so many of our Episcopal prayers are no more and no less than words of the Bible stitched together. As I put it in the book, there are biblical words and extrabiblical words in our Episcopal prayers. The extrabiblical words are, to use a culinary metaphor, binding agents. They are like tapioca in a blueberry pie. The tapioca thickens around the berries and holds them together. But the berries are the main point.

Before writing *A Word to Live By*, I knew in some general way that a lot of our prayers use scriptural phrases, but I'd never really stepped back to think about that. And frankly, when I do step back to think about it, it seems strange. If prayer is primarily speaking back to God the words God gave us in Scripture, then . . . well, what does that say about what prayer is? What are we doing when we do that particular thing? I thought about this a lot while I was writing, and I'm still thinking about it.

There's the idea (borrowed from the world of drama) of "allo-repetiton": repeating back to someone what she has said first. So we might use a word our friend has just used, or we might repeat her entire sentence with tiny modifications. When your friend says, "Do you want to know what happened to me today?" you don't reply, "Yes." You reply, "I *do* want to know what happened to you today!" When we allo-repeat, we're showing that we're paying attention to our friend, and, ultimately, by borrowing her speech, we strengthen and cement our bond to her. Our habit of borrowing God's words when speaking to God might be a sign, an agent, of our intimacy with God.

I think allo-repetiton is a very good framework for thinking about praying the words of Scripture back to God. But I'm sure there's more to say. I hope readers will come up with their own ideas about what's happening for us when we pray all these scripturally-saturated prayers.

Stephanie: *I'm glad so much of what you wrote still resonates for you. I wonder . . . which part of the story you would change?*

Lauren: In part because of the book's length, I didn't write a chapter on interpretation—stating clearly that Scripture is always being interpreted, it's not self-evident and it doesn't interpret itself, and interpretations are going to be different in different times and in different communities. I wish I had.

Stephanie: *What would you say now?*

There's a bit of a throw-away on page 8, about the metaphorical language Scripture uses to describe itself: the Bible tells us the Bible is a running path, and a lamp, and a snowy landscape. I wish I'd taken more space to explore those metaphors. I think they each offer a powerful picture of what the Bible is, and what kind of thing it is to read the Bible. I hope that any groups who read *A Word to Live By* might take some time to discuss

> What metaphors would you invoke to describe the Bible or reading the Bible? Is it like a running path, a lamp along the road, a snowy landscape, a tasty meal, or something else? Why do you experience it that way?

what those metaphors suggest about Bible reading. And I might make that the topic of my next book!

Finally, as I said a minute ago, any summary of Scripture tells you more about the person summarizing than it does about the Bible itself. I am struck that my summary in Chapter 2 includes less than a sentence about the twenty-three books of the New Testament that follow the Gospels; less than a sentence, in other words, about the establishment of the church after the ascension of Jesus. I don't know that I'd change that. In the Episcopal Church, we focus so little on the Old Testament that I think it's usefully provocative to have a summary of the Bible that is mostly a summary of the Old Testament. And yet, perhaps a bit more needs to be said about what the Bible has to say about the church-after-ascension.

Stephanie: *You're a college professor, so you spend a lot of time with younger generations. I wonder ... what you would highlight if you were a companion walking with someone under age thirty or maybe even new to the church?*

Lauren: On page 10, I quote Anselm of Canterbury's instructions to chew the honeycomb of Jesus' words in Scripture, to taste their goodness, to lap up the Bible like the most delicious cocktail.

Stephanie: *Did you really just compare drinking in Scripture to drinking a yummy cocktail?*

Lauren: I guess I did! I love this set of instructions, because it reminds us that Scripture is delicious—delightful—that it's for our enjoyment as much as for our instruction. To be sure, I don't always enjoy Scripture or find it delicious. But maybe when we don't find it enjoyable—when we find it boring, or when we find it offensive—we can take a leaf from the art critic Peter Schjeldahl. He once said that when he looks at a painting he does not like, he asks himself, "What would I like about this if I liked it?" Perhaps a question to bring to a passage of Scripture is "What would I delight in if I delighted in something? What would I find delectable if I found something delectable?"

Chapter 8

A Conversation on Worship with Jeffrey Lee and Dent Davidson

"The liturgy is not a performance. The liturgy is an art form that is not meant to entertain or impress or edify or instruct. It is a corporate act of the people of God that aims to change us, to draw us out of our self-conscious preoccupations and deeper into the mystery of the dying and rising love of God for us and for this world. It is an encounter with God's own presence." *

Jeffrey Lee and Dent Davidson were clear in *Gathered for God* that they weren't writing a book about the Prayer Book. Their volume is about what the Prayer Book makes possible: the kind of community that takes God seriously and gathers to "pray like we mean it." They structured the book in part to follow the experience of Eucharist, the primary worship gathering for Episcopalians. It opens with an introduction to that most human of acts, ritual, and then flows into hospitality, story, offering,

---

* Jeffrey Lee and Dent Davidson, *Gathered for God,* vol. 8, Church's Teachings for a Changing World (New York: Church Publishing, 2018), 77.

feeding, sending, singing, and bathing (also known as baptism). Their deep camaraderie has grown over decades working together as clergy (Jeff is the bishop of the Diocese of Chicago) and musician (Dent is the diocese's missioner for liturgy and music and music chaplain to the Episcopal House of Bishops). That partnership informed their conversation with Eric.

Eric: *What part of the book do you each like best?*

Jeff: I like that we saved baptism for nearly the ending—the end is the beginning. It's counter-intuitive but purposeful.

Dent: I love how the book is framed in story from beginning to end. Telling our own stories helps us tell the Great Story with passion and personal impact. We began with the "running race" story and ended with baptism. Stories are powerful and deeply liturgical. Baptism is not inclusion but expulsion; we are gathered in to be sent out to change things.

Jeff: I also like the way we talk about open communion [the practice of welcoming anyone to the table, regardless of whether they are Episcopal or even baptized]. When we talk in the church about what is allowed or not, it often is a dead-end conversation; it doesn't get you anywhere. Here, we explore an example where a church found a way to invite people away from the altar as profound hospitality. I love coming to the topic sideways. Instead of asking whether this is right or wrong, we ask, Have you thought about this?

This is not a how-to book, but a "why-to" book. Why do we give ourselves to this? Why do we have to take in and go out? So much of the conversation on liturgical matters just bores me to tears. I don't care about whether this or that is permissible. More importantly, I care about two different questions. The first is: What do you think you are doing? What do you think a newcomer thinks when you are waving your hands over the altar frantically? Bishop Neil Alexander

> As you engage in worship, try asking two questions:
>
> 1. What do you think you are doing?
> 2. What are you doing?

says the minute you step into the room as a presider or musician, the assembly is exegeting (that is, reading and interpreting the text of) your body. What are they reading?

The second question is: What are you doing? This question is different from the former one. We might think one thing and what other people get might be very different. People put meaning on things with zero backup except what they did last year. Nothing is wrong except when it becomes a sacred cow.

Dent: Part of our work and our play is to identify "liturgical sacred cows," those elements that may have little or no meaning in twenty-first century worship, but no one dares to mess with. In one workshop, people were invited to inscribe the sacred cows on paper and then launch them on the "cattlepult." One by one, sacred cows went flying—it was our collective, symbolic letting go. I loved telling that story. I loved being part of setting people free like that.

Eric: What part of the book is the most important to you?

Dent: Right now the Holy Spirit has lit a fire under me about going out and engaging in evangelism, so the concept of sending is really important to me. For the last ten years or more, I have been less a musician and more of a missioner. It's one of the things the church doesn't take seriously enough, in my opinion. I hope this book might help to change the minds of some leaders, and that they emphasize how we are witnesses to Jesus after we leave the building on Sunday mornings.

Jeff: This book is not about liturgy but what liturgy is for—namely, mission. People shouldn't just be comfortable about saying the word "Jesus." They should be passionate in saying it. When was the last time you gasped out loud in an act of worship because something so holy was happening right in front of your face? Our baptismal identity—to participate in the death and resurrection of Jesus—is a life-altering reality, whether you realize it or not. It's the single most important thing that can happen to a person. So why is baptism in most parishes almost like an afterthought? Most baptism is not presented as a life-changing experience.

Dent: Bishop Tom Breidenthal said baptism is being expelled out of the womb into the world. In order for creation to be, God has to rend God's own being. We need a rending in order for there to be something new. Baptism is where it all happens.

Eric: You've painted some vivid pictures just now. I wonder . . . does this mean there are parts of the book you would change, given where our society is now?

Dent: We would consider changing the title of the book, since it doesn't say anything about sending.

Jeff: We also would add a section on the church as a community of resistance. We are moving more into post-Christendom.

It is now in full display. People have basic questions about what is prayer and what does it mean. For example, in our diocese, we had lively debates about whether or not to pray for the president by name in our liturgy. There isn't a lot of compelling, helpful theology guiding whether we do this or not. And of course, all this is a window into a larger question: What does it mean to be in and not of the world?

Dent: What does it mean to be a community of resistance if we believe our vows at baptism, that we will respect the dignity of every human being? Donald J. Trump is not exempted. The fact I have a problem praying for him is not his problem; it's mine. Liturgy can lead me into a deeper state of being a follower of Jesus by forcing me to deal with questions like "I am going to pray for whom?"

Jeff: Another thing: so often, when we renew and revive the liturgy, it becomes an intellectual discourse rather than a vehicle for discovering and sharing the diverse prayers of the assembly. We should be praying the liturgy and sinking deep in it and allowing the liturgy to shape us.

A well-written Eucharistic prayer will do that. The act of receiving communion will do that if we allow it to. We are afraid of the inherent power of liturgical elements, so we trivialize them. We fear drowning in the water of baptism, and we should; baptism is dangerous. The world we live in pushes us deeper into our roots, which are profoundly liturgical. The liturgy shapes and forms us. The liturgy is in us. It forms us and sends us out. It moves us deeper into being God's people every week.

As the world gets meaner and stingier, we need to get deeper, higher, and more generous and lavish. We don't need to invent new stuff. We are loaded with riches. We just don't mine deeply enough from what we already have. That's why I'm not very enthusiastic about revision of the Prayer Book—I don't think we are done mining the depth of the current book. Now, I'm not starting a society to preserve the 1979 Prayer Book, but I really would rather apply my energy to push us deeper into living what we already have.

Eric: Certainly a lot of new and young people come into our church and find the Prayer Book refreshing and surprising. What you would highlight if you were a companion walking with a younger person or someone who is new to the faith?

Dent: We are a couple of white guys. This is a predominantly white church. We don't spend nearly enough time on the offerings of non-white communities. Even though we've both had experiences in Latino, Hispanic and black communities, we don't bring those voices to the book. Sometimes, we have to shut up and listen. The story we have is incomplete because we haven't heard the stories of others who are culturally different from us. It is through hearing their stories that I can be a true brother or sister, a true companion.

Jeff: In the road to Emmaus story, Jesus didn't do a lot of talking at first. Instead, he asked them to tell their stories. After hearing their stories, he broke open the Scriptures for them and then they shared the breaking of the bread—also another rending. Gordon Lathrop said that in order for any symbol to be reliably Christian, it has to be broken.

Therefore, as a companion, I would first ask them, "What's *your* story?" And I would listen. Then I'd tell some of my story, and then find ways to relate both of our stories to the Great Story: how all of these ultimately tell of God's amazing love for us and for all of creation. And then I'd invite them to continue telling, and living into what's next in the Great Story, which is still being written.

Dent: And I suppose it would be nice if we could share the message from the end of the first chapter:

> When we gather for worship, it is not simply to share some interesting ideas about God or fond theories regarding what we might make of Jesus. We gather in the presence of God. We gather to meet, to receive, to share in the life, death, and resurrection of Jesus himself. And we do this the way he taught us by his own example: at table, in the breaking and sharing of bread, in a cup of wine, passed from hand to hand.*

I hope we can make that clear to them. It is truly good news.

---

* Lee and Davidson, xiii.

PART II

Practicing the Way of Companionship and Conversation

The Episcopal Way is more than facts and doctrine. It's a way of life that leads us into deeper relationship with each other, with God and with our neighbors. Especially today, when faith has in many instances been turned into a wedge separating us from one another, the Episcopal Way draws us more deeply into companionship, conversation, and communion.

In the chapters that follow, we explore practical approaches to growing relationship and dialogue in ever-widening circles: walking and talking with God, with our own truest selves, with community, with tradition, with neighbors and with "the enemy" in whom we may very well see God, which sends us back around the circle again. The Episcopal Way truly becomes real when we walk and talk it out in community.

Chapter 9

Walking and Talking with God

"John 3:16"

Bumper stickers announce it. So do billboards at most football stadiums in America. Stephanie's best friend has it patched onto one of his skullcaps. She recently discovered it on the label of her favorite dress.

John 3:16 may be the most familiar Scripture citation of all time. You can see it everywhere, which means it's easy to miss how stunning and scandalous the passage is.

If this is true—"God so loved the world that he gave his only Son, so that everyone who believes in him may not perish but may have eternal life"—there are serious implications. God isn't the distant parent you can never please or get to know. God is holding nothing back. God squanders love like the prodigal son squanders his loot. God longs, yearns, needs, hopes. God *is* love.

God loves us so much that God has chosen to be known to us in the three persons of the Trinity: the Father, the Son and the Holy Spirit, also experienced as Creator, Redeemer, and

Sustainer. The Trinity is in ongoing conversation and relationship within Godself *and* with us. We, in turn, can draw near to God.

Emmanuel: God Is with Us

How do we approach becoming companions with God? It starts with realizing you don't have to work for this relationship. God started the movement. True, every relationship is two-way, but God is already walking down the Emmaus Road with us or running off the front porch to welcome us home. Our work is not to find or to woo God. Our task, our practice, is to draw nearer and shape our lives around the abundant, radiant love that's been waiting since the beginning of time.

The Episcopal Way of following Jesus starts from this admittedly positive place. If other Christian traditions find their center at the Crucifixion, our way is at least as focused on the Incarnation, that scandalous moment when the Word who existed before time "became flesh and dwelt among us" (John 1). Episcopalians assume that moment was the ultimate game-changer: because God has dwelt with us as Immanuel, because flesh and spirit have entered into perfect union in Christ, nothing is impossible.

We also trust Jesus meant it when he promised to continue sending his Spirit and drawing near us. Those flashes of presence and light could be understood as sacraments: "a visible, physical sign of the still-lively presence of Jesus, usually housed in a ritual like baptism or communion, both moments when we believe Jesus shows up to meet his followers." In *The Episcopal Way*, we called on the words of Thomas Cranmer, architect of the Prayer Book, who describes his own experience of intimacy with Jesus via the sacraments:

> Our Savior Christ hath not only set forth these things most plainly in his holy word, that we may hear them with our ears, but he has also ordained one visible sacrament of spiritual regeneration in water [*baptism*], and another visible sacrament of spiritual nourishment in bread and wine [*communion*], to the intent that, as much as is possible for man, we may see Christ with our eyes, smell him at our nose, taste him with our mouths, grope him with our hands, and perceive him with all our senses.

We can meet Christ in the bread, in the wine, in the waters. In Christ, God has already stepped forth to be our companion on the Way.

Love on a Two-Way Street

What a relief it is, to know we're not trying to lure God out of hiding, and to trust that God's love is the one guarantee in an otherwise capricious universe. As Michael Curry has noted, we're not placing God at the center; we're moving ourselves out of the center, so we can see God in the place God has been all along.

Still . . . have you ever been in love? Or nurtured a close friendship, especially at a distance? Then you know relationship is two-way. If you don't make time for the relationship, no amount of love from the other person is going to sustain it. If anything, one-sided relationships have a way of festering and causing resentment on both sides. God has already committed to being our companion. How do we turn and become closer companions to God?

Name God

Granted, human beings don't have the best track record with putting names to God. Still Jesus asked his disciples to try when he said, "Who do you say that I am?" (Matthew 16:15). He knew it's all but impossible to be in relationship with someone whose name and image you do not know. So who do you say God is, for you? Reflect for some time on the question.

> Who do you say God is, for you? What images have you associated with God in the past? How do you imagine God now?

1. What was your first image of God? What did God look and sound like to you, in your earliest memory of God?

2. Is there an image or passage from Scripture that resonates for you today? What is it? What feelings do you experience when you recall this image or passage? How do you talk to the God you see and imagine?

Notice God

Jonathan Myers, a priest friend of ours in Spokane, Washington, has spent lots of time with "New Monastics": contemporary, often younger communities that adapt monastic traditions for life today, including communal living and crafting a Rule of Life to help to shape a group's prayer, behaviors, and choices. Myers encourages people to take up the practice of simply noticing God in these ways:

LOOK: The presence of God is within and around us, waiting to be recognized. Where do you see God when you look . . .

- at your own life and story—as Frederick Buechner suggests, "Listen to your life. See it for the fathomless mystery it is."*

- at your community—What fills your heart with gladness? Where does your heart sink?

- at the internet and social media—What sites, groups, individuals reflect the loving, liberating presence of God?

LISTEN: Be quiet and hear the still, small voice of God. Where do you hear God when you listen . . .

- to yourself—to your own wisdom and to God speaking in you

- to others—to another person's pain or joy or insight

- for the "it"—to whatever comes to life in the space between/among you and other people

Track God

One of the best tools for noticing or tracking where God has showed up on the journey with you is a spiritual autobiography. Think through the major moments in your life when you have felt close to God and perhaps when you've felt distant from God. Pay special attention to the highs, lows, and major turning points in your overall life story. For each major encounter—or struggle—with God, place a mark on a page and write a few words or an image that captures what happened.

---

* Frederick Buechner, *Now and Then: A Memoir of Vocation* (San Francisco: Harper & Row, 1983), 87.

When you've got your timeline, go back and study the God-moments. See if you can recall the stories for each moment:

- Remember the details: what you saw, felt, smelled, tasted, who was there, where you were, how old you were, etc.

- Keep it real: there's no need to use specialized language or to sound like an expert

- Listen to your own life and trust your experience

- Focus on God: Peer past "I felt peaceful," and ask what made you sense you were *with God* in that moment? What are the signs of the loving presence of God—the Creator, Son and/or Spirit—with you?

Feel free to write up the stories in a journal, maybe over an afternoon, maybe during a few sittings. Read back through when you're finished. Do you notice any patterns? When and how do you most often feel God with you? Ask God for more of what you experienced with God in these moments.

Pray to God

Episcopalians are people of prayer. We pray from books, in gathered worship, without words in the predawn silence. However it manifests, our tradition trusts the power of prayer.

The Benedictine monastic path has shaped much of our common life, which keeps us coming back to the rhythm of daily prayer known as the Daily Office. We've adapted the monastic tradition of praying from nine to five times a day, and our Prayer Book features a variety of forms for offering Morning Prayer, Noonday Prayer, and Evening Prayer, as well as Compline before turning in for the night. The Prayer Book is also filled with prayers we call "collects": prayers in a particular form that gather up (or "collect") the concerns for a particular occasion and offer them to God.

Those formal prayers are dear to the Episcopal heart. But don't let all the prescribed words fool you. Prayer isn't merely speaking words to God. Prayer is opening the channel for communication between us and God. As Jeffrey Lee and Dent Davidson offered in their volume on worship, *Gathered for God*: "[W]e are not performing a pageant or a play so that God will notice and delight in us."* If our hope is to enter into deeper relationship with the God who longs for us, then prayer is one of the main ways we say "yes" to God's overture.

Monastics may once again be our guides for developing a personal, prayerful relationship with God. The brothers of the Society of St. John the Evangelist, an Episcopal Benedictine order based in Cambridge, Massachusetts, have for more than a hundred years guided people into deeper union with God in a changing world. In 2017, they launched a special project in partnership with the worldwide Anglican Communion Office called Thy Kingdom Come (find it at www.thykingdomcome.global).

This online campaign stirred and equipped Anglicans to "deepen their friendship with Jesus, bring others to know Jesus or know him better, and come to know that every aspect of their life is the stuff of prayer." They offered daily modules designed to help individuals and communities to pray in these ways:

- Day 1: I pray to you . . .

- Day 2: I praise you . . .

---

* Lee and Davidson, 84

- Day 3: I give thanks . . .
- Day 4: I am sorry . . .
- Day 5: I offer to you . . .
- Day 6: I pray for . . .
- Day 7: I ask your help . . .
- Day 8: I adore you . . .
- Day 9: I celebrate . . .
- Day 10: I enter into your silence . . .
- Day 11: I do this in your name . . ./I pray that your kingdom will come

Most of us are familiar with prayers like Day 3 (thanksgiving) or Day 4 (sorry). Who can make it through the day without the theme of Day 7 (help!)? As you deepen relationship with God, you may appreciate having a wider variety of ways to talk and listen and simply dwell with God. Human relationships presume that kind of variety—think of Gary Chapman's *The Five Love Languages* and how helpful it is to have multiple ways of expressing and building a more loving relationship. Thy Kingdom Come offers a concrete way for us to expand our vocabulary for communicating with God.

Our friend Carrie Boren Headington likes to point out in her talks that Jesus is and was God among us, and even he prayed constantly. Before he preached, before he chose the twelve apostles, before he healed the sick, before he taught the Beatitudes, before he was crucified—Jesus prayed. Clearly, prayer is not an admission that God is not with you. Prayer is answering God's knock and saying, "I'm here, too. And I'm listening."

Show Up with God

We spoke earlier of the sacraments of baptism and Eucharist, those visible signs of the invisible grace of God. Many Episcopalians will say we believe all of life is sacramental, that is, capable of revealing or bearing the grace of God. The Holy One is no doubt waiting and longing for us everywhere, if we have eyes to see.

For many of us, meditating on Scripture is a primary way to meet God. One summer, Stephanie set herself the task of reading the entire Bible—Genesis 1 to Revelation 22. She even captured the noteworthy passages on notecards and filled two boxes with her homemade set of Bible flashcards. It started as a project; by the end of the summer, she enjoyed deeper relationship with the God whose story unfolds in the pages of Scripture. Today, when she charts her own spiritual autobiography, that summer stands out as a high point.

When Eric served on a diocesan staff, he made a habit of studying Scripture with church leaders, usually focusing on the lessons from the Revised Common Lectionary for the upcoming Sunday. The biblical lesson had an uncanny habit of speaking directly to the church's struggles. Time after time, he saw groups experiencing Scripture as more than history, more than someone else's story. The Bible became a companion introducing them to God's actions and God's yearning . . . and helping them to align their own lives with the dream of God.

There are many more focused spaces and moments where we are likely to meet and nurture communion with God:

> What are the two places, activities or practices that lead you close to God, or make you more aware of God's nearness to you?

- Bible study
- Worship
- Personal prayer
- Group prayer
- Christian community and fellowship
- Retreats
- Group intensives (such as Cursillo)
- Revival
- Service and action

We can choose to place ourselves in those spaces and to make time for those moments. God is ready to be our companion. These choices communicate that we long just as much to be companions with God.

Chapter 10

Walking and Talking with Yourself

> So when you are offering your gift at the altar, if you remember that your brother or sister has something against you, leave your gift there before the altar and go; first be reconciled to your brother or sister, and then come and offer your gift. —Matthew 5:23–24

A few years back, Eric took part in an intensive Bible study with eminent scholar Walter Wink. After they sat with the above text, Wink asked each participant to imagine walking toward a holy place with a gift in hand, only to discover someone standing in the way.

At that point, Wink asked each participant to set up two chairs: one for the self and a second one symbolizing the person who had something against them. To work out the issue, you had to sit in the chairs alternately, having a conversation between yourself and the pretend-other. Eric initially thought it a silly exercise, but he gave it a try. As he moved between the voice of self and other, he came to a surprising conclusion: the struggle wasn't really with the other; it was with the part of himself that he didn't like.

By acknowledging his own internal conflict, Eric found he could reconcile with the person in his imaginary dialogue (later, he went to the person in real life and found a way toward healing). Through that experience, he discovered the imaginary gift he most longed to offer to God was not some great strength, but his own weakness.

Courageous Conversations

Being a companion to yourself on the journey with Jesus takes more courage and care than you might think. Some of us have a surprisingly hard time acknowledging the parts of ourselves that we like, feel good about, or feel proud of. After all, isn't Christianity about humility and self-sacrifice? Luke 1:51–52 celebrates the God who has "scattered the proud in the thoughts of their hearts" and "brought down the powerful from their thrones, and lifted up the lowly." If that is the fate of the proud, no one wants to risk looking too confident.

On the other hand, few of us know how to cultivate healthy ways of relating to the parts of ourselves that we're ashamed of or even angry at. It's easier to wall off the sensitive territory, hide our faults and vulnerability, maybe not even admit it to ourselves. Some of us are tempted to wallow in our unworthiness, to the point where not even God's love can penetrate the fog of self-recrimination.

That isn't God's will for humanity. God redeems and welcomes home all the parts of you: the good, the bad, the beautiful, the ugly, and everything in between. If you doubt this, spend some time reflecting on the final section of the Great Commandment (Matthew 22:37–40 or Mark 12:28–31). Jesus says love God and love your neighbor *as yourself*. If you can't offer compassion, curiosity, grace, attention, and genuine love to your whole self, you might end up projecting what you don't love about yourself onto others.

You Are Beloved

Stephanie begins trainings on a host of topics with what she calls a "Belovedness Meditation." In her experience, if people start with the truth of our belovedness before God and allow that love to infuse the way we regard ourselves, we tend to be more receptive and generative with whatever teaching and practice comes next.

So she begins with a reading of the Luke account of Jesus's baptism:

> Now when all the people were baptized, and when Jesus also had been baptized and was praying, the heaven was opened, and the Holy Spirit descended upon him in bodily form like a dove. And a voice came from heaven, "You are my Son, the Beloved; with you I am well pleased." (Luke 3:21–22)

The group will then dwell for a few moments in the silence. Eventually she rings a bell and asks them to repeat, silently or aloud: "You are my child, the Beloved. With you I am well pleased." Participants say it enough times to get uncomfortable, and then to get comfortable, and then to truly hear not their own voice but God's voice proclaiming this fundamental truth.

It is worth taking that message in, on a regular basis, and practicing living as if we really are beloved. Because once you receive the inevitability and fullness of that love, anything is possible. Just look at what happened to Jesus. After Jesus received his baptism and blessing, his belovedness was like a jet-pack on his back, propelling him out to launch his ministry of healing, teaching, organizing, truth-telling, loving, and giving his life for love of the world.

With a clear grounding in your own belovedness, you can be more like Jesus: more generous, more prayerful, more daring in offering love and welcome to others. You can enter the scariest situations, embrace the most daunting challenges, and bear peace. Why? Because you are wrapped in the love of the one who made the world.

Henri Nouwen was a Catholic priest, spiritual director, and Ivy League scholar, and he struggled to receive his own belovedness. Eventually he made a drastic shift and moved to live and work in the L'Arche Community with people with profound disabilities and an even more profound capacity to love. That's when he learned the truth: "God's words, 'You are my Beloved' reveal the most intimate truth about all human beings. Alas, the ultimate spiritual temptation is to doubt this fundamental truth about ourselves."[*]

"You are my Beloved." Imagine God saying these words to you. It might be even easier, then, to imagine God holding every one whom God has made with the same loving, patient regard.

If there is one word people tend to equate with Episcopalians, it might just be "nonjudgmental." As Scott Bader-Saye

---

[*] Henri Nouwen, *Spiritual Direction: Wisdom for the Long Journey of Faith* (New York: HarperOne, 2006), 28.

said earlier in this volume, following Jesus on the Episcopal Way does not begin with repudiating the bad or sinful parts of ourselves or of the world. We're on a holistic journey. In facing and embracing our shadow and our light, and holding all that before God in love, we become whole. We also become more able to be gracious companions and conversation partners with the diverse peoples around us.

Chapter 11

Walking and Talking with Community

One might expect church to be a natural place for finding deep companionship with God and one another. After all, theologian Michael Battle points out, "The *imago dei*, the image of God, is community. Our uniqueness as individuals matters for sure, but we are individuals in community."* But every congregation is a divine and human institution, powered by the Spirit and enacted by human beings with all our limitations.

What makes the difference? How do you shift from being a group to becoming community? How do people go from traveling side by side to being companions? In the Outline of the Faith at the close of the Book of Common Prayer, we state the mission of the Episcopal Church: to "restore all people to union with God and each other in Christ." Maybe one of the best ways to live into that promise is by sharing our stories. As the Beloved Community Story-Sharing Guidebook explains:

---

* Michael Battle, "God's Kind of Apocalypse," sermon preached October 8, 2017 (http://day1.org/7978-michael_battle_gods_kind_of_apocalypse).

The work of stories is slow and humble stuff. This work is soul-to-soul, person-to-person, heart-to-heart. Through story we are able to see, hear, and learn about ourselves, about the Holy, and the things that are most important in life. Stories are what communities and churches are made of.*

Becoming Real

For Stephanie, there's nothing like witnessing the moment when people who have spent years together in church discover each other's stories for the first time. They have attended meetings, read books, made major decisions, worshiped at the same altar rail. They have shared communion but they are not yet companions. Time and again, stories are the vehicle that carries people to the other side.

Members of the Episcopal Evangelism Team witness that "ah-ha" moment on a fairly regular basis. They lead an exercise called Cardboard Testimonies,** adapted from evangelical communities more familiar with personal storytelling. The exercise is a simple one that works with a class, a congregation, a workshop or a whole church convention.

- Quietly recall a time in your life when you struggled deeply. Then ponder the movement toward healing, reconciliation, resolution and/or light.

---

* Episcopal Church Evangelism and Reconciliation Ministries, "Beloved Community StorySharing Guidebook," (https://www.episcopalchurch.org/files/documents/beloved_community_storysharing_guidebook_reader_single_pages_0.pdf), page 5.

** Find Cardboard Testimonies in the Evangelism 101 handouts, available at www.episcopalchurch.org/evangelismtoolkit.

- After this time for reflection, take the provided cardboard and marker and write in large print just a few words to capture the experience. On one side of the cardboard, five to seven words that narrate the struggle; on the other side, narrate resurrection. Be aware that others will see your cardboard.

- Then take your cardboard and mill around the room. Pause with someone. Hold up your cardboard for your partner to read—one side, turn to the other. Your partner holds up her cardboard—one side, turn to the other. Then you both offer some spontaneous gesture that acknowledges what you feel as you witness each other's journeys. It could be a handshake, a nod, a hug, a bow, a grin, a tear, an "Amen."

- After that largely silent witnessing, each person moves to a new partner and repeats. Keep moving about the room, so that everyone experiences the exchange with several others.

- After five minutes or so of moving and sharing in relative silence, you will match up in pairs. Make sure everyone has just one partner.

- Partner A takes about a minute to share the story of his card, offering up the painful side and the hopeful side while Partner B graciously receives it. Then trade roles, so Partner B becomes the speaker, and Partner A receives the gift of B's story.

- At the conclusion of the exchange, both partners should offer some spontaneous gesture that acknowledges what you feel as you hear each other's journeys.

- Time permitting, the whole group can debrief the experience.

Groups of almost every size and configuration seem to come alive during this exercise. In one troubled diocese, a group of eighty people from several congregations had gathered for an evangelism workshop. Pain was everywhere; the church space itself had been the site of emotional violence and abuse. And yet, as people began to hold up their cards and tell their stories, the room began to vibrate with energy, curiosity, and something else: hope. As the exercise continued, some people hugged. Some did high-fives. With the stories came tears and amazement at what God had brought each of them through.

When the group debriefed the exercise, one elder stood and said, "You have no idea. We were taught not to trust each other. I've been sitting next to him in the pews for twenty years and I didn't know what he's been through, where he's seen God. We needed this." They discovered what we all sometimes forget: that Christians, and especially Episcopalians, can only do faith in community. Stories are a huge part of how we forge those bonds.

Space for the Story

There is nothing so unique about Cardboard Testimonies. The point is creating intentional spaces for offering and holding each other's stories. The Beecken Center at Sewanee School of Theology trains people in how to hold those spaces using the Living in the Green discernment curriculum. Community organizers rely on one-to-one relational meetings: brief, contained conversations where two people talk about their deepest passions and greatest hopes and discover common cause. The Kaleidoscope Institute leads Gracious and Courageous Conversations, a process for groups to share stories on difficult topics (see the chapter on "Walking and Talking with My Enemy"). The Episcopal Church's Beloved Community Story-Sharing Campaign trains people to share and receive stories of faith, race, and difference.

All these storytelling methodologies and more help groups to deepen relationship with God and with each other. Once the group creates shared space for vulnerable, authentic presence, where we see God in each other and God in the space between us, we can take risks and grow in love like never before.

Eric likes to call this a "space for grace." Ronald Heifetz calls it a holding environment: the secure, consistent, dependable, structured relationships and practices that provide an anchor so we can make the adaptive moves necessary to actually deal with change. Holding environments and gracious spaces take many shapes: counselor and client, teacher or class and student, coach or team and player, priest or church community and members.

These gracious spaces tend to be marked by certain principles and practices:

- *Vulnerable and real*: There's a famous scene in *Indiana Jones and the Last Crusade*, when our hero stands at the precipice, danger on his heels, a vast chasm in front of him. He takes a step into thin air . . . and the bridge appears. Community is like that. Someone has to take that first step out onto space and give others the chance to form a web. If we share our stories with vulnerability and authenticity and hold the space for others to do the same, they just might.

- *Mutual*: If one person does all the sharing, it's an interview. To form genuine relationship, both have to share what's real and true. One person may model it, but eventually it takes two.

- *Regular*: Mutual story-telling can become part of the church's life. After a while, people expect it to happen in sermons, at coffee hour, in leadership meetings, in small groups.

- *Beyond dialogue*: Dialogue implies that there are two sides and they may or may not truly touch. Sometimes, that's the most you can hope for. Communities move further, toward conversation and conversion. I expect that I will be changed or grow by what I hear from you, and vice versa.

- *Rooted in love*: Companions in community ultimately wonder, How shall we love? How do we all move toward wholeness? How does God want to use me to grow you into what God intends you to be?

- *Rooted in curiosity*: Communities don't require uniformity. When there's diversity of thought, culture, or experience within our community, it's not a roadblock. It's an opportunity to become more curious than ever and to return to our stories. Instead of wondering, "What do you think?" try asking, "What in your life has led you to believe or see what you do?"

Steps on the Way

There's no guaranteed formula for cultivating loving Christian community. Jesus begged his disciples to "love one another as I have loved you" (John 15:12). Paul offers a few more insights in his letter to the Romans, where he writes:

Let love be genuine; hate what is evil, hold fast to what is good; love one another with mutual affection; outdo one another in showing honor. Live in harmony with one another; do not be haughty, but associate with the lowly; do not claim to be wiser than you are. Do not repay anyone evil for evil, but take thought for what is noble in the sight of all. If it is possible, so far as it depends on you, live peaceably with all. (Romans 12:9–10, 16–18)

In the day-to-day life of a community, we have seen these practices bringing Christians into deeper loving relationship with each other and fortifying them for living as the body of Christ in the world.

- *Share your stories.* Congregations create a storytelling culture by regularly carving out space for sharing around simple questions:
  —When did you first discover this church? What drew you to this community?
  —At what moment did you decide you would stay here? What keeps you in this community?
  —Name a moment when you truly saw God alive in this community.

- *Share the preaching.* Preachers can ask a simple, clear question in the midst of the sermon and invite people to share in small groups for one minute per person.

- *Read Scripture together.* It's powerful to get to know the story of God with God's people through sacred history by studying the Bible together. Use simple tools like Dwelling in the Word or the African Bible Study.

- *Pray together*. Individually, in worship, in small groups, before and after every community gathering. For help deepening your prayer, look to Chapter 9: Walking and Talking with God.

- *Gather a group to write personal spiritual autobiographies*. Imagine telling your stories, stretched out as a narrative tracing God's presence and activity in your life. Move from your earliest recollections to your most recent, noticing when you've experienced God's nearness and when you've felt distant from God. For more on this practice, go to page 67.

- *Create a community spiritual autobiography*. When have you as a group experienced genuine intimacy with God? When have you experienced barrenness as a community seeking God? What seemed to make the difference in each instance?

Chapter 12

Walking and Talking with the Neighborhood

Celebrant: Will you seek and serve Christ in
all persons, loving your neighbor
as yourself?

People: I will, with God's help.

Every Wednesday morning St. Mary's Cathedral in Memphis serves up breakfast and worship with homeless and hungry people. That's not so unusual among churches. But at St. Mary's, homeless participants also help to decide what food gets cooked, how it will be served, and how the worship service will flow.

St. Mary's leaders Roger and Margery Wolcott have taken another radical step forward. They rented a house a block away from St. Mary's and called it Constance Abbey. Roger and Margery provide a daily liturgy of morning and evening prayers. Every week, they personally host dinner with a few homeless people and a few Cathedral members (yes, there's sometimes crossover). In these neighborly conversations over a meal, people discover stories, hopes, and needs everyone shares. For instance, St. Mary's leaders learned how hard it is to find a place to shower and wash if you have no home. So they rented another house next door and open it every morning so people with no home can come in, take a shower, do laundry and most importantly be in community.

Constance Abbey isn't a social service center. Members of the community sign up to handle the house's upkeep: cleaning, gardening, etc. Church members come and build relationship with those who might elsewhere be considered "guests." And if a homeless person in the Constance Abbey orbit gets withheld by the criminal justice system, church leaders will accompany them to court. Inevitably, the judge asks who the church guests are. The refrain is the same: "We are from Constance Abbey, and we are friends."

St. Mary's is living into a contemporary vision of companionship and partnership with all our neighbors. What if other followers of Jesus took a page from the same book?

Who Is My Neighbor?

The relationship starts with a simple question: Who are your neighbors? Demographic patterns show that most Americans live in rather homogenous zones. In other words, our neighbors generally share similar economic status, cultural backgrounds, values, beliefs, etc. In the Gospel of Matthew, Jesus asked us to stretch further.

> For if you love those who love you, what reward do you have? Do not even the tax collectors do the same? And if you greet only your brothers and sisters, what more are you doing than others? Do not even the Gentiles do the same? Be

perfect, therefore, as your heavenly Father is perfect. (Matthew 5:46–48)

Eric learned an interesting fact about this passage in a different course with biblical scholar Walter Wink. In Aramaic, the language Jesus spoke, "perfect" does not mean "flawless." The closest translation for "perfect" is "wholeness" or "completeness." So a more accurate translation of Matthew 5:48 might read, "Be inclusive (or comprehensive) as your heavenly Father is inclusive (or comprehensive)."

If we isolate ourselves in enclaves of people who are just like us, we will not know the whole truth of what God is doing in our wider communities. We need to meet and get to know neighbors who seem the same and neighbors who are markedly different, especially those who lack the same structural privilege and power.

Anglicans and Episcopalians ought to resonate with this approach. It is, after all, the heart of the Via Media, one of the first principles of the Episcopal Way. We seek the truth between extremes, not necessarily the middle but a measured and discerning path that listens to the wisdom on what appear to be opposing sides.

Another way of naming this value is to say we are "comprehensive." In 1968 the Lambeth Conference, the every-ten-years meeting of bishops from across the worldwide Anglican Communion, issued a statement that describes the concept well:

Comprehensiveness demands agreement on fundamentals, while tolerating disagreement on matters in which Christians may differ without feeling the necessity of breaking communion. In the mind of an Anglican, comprehensiveness is not compromise. Nor is it to bargain one truth for another. It is not a sophisticated word for syncretism. Rather it implies that the apprehension of truth is a growing thing; we only gradually succeed in "knowing the truth." For we believe that in leading us into the truth the Holy Spirit may have some surprises in store for us in the future as he has had in the past.*

Episcopalians should be among the first to step out and get to know our neighbors. This is how we come to fully understand what God is up to, who God is, who we are and what we are up to with God.

Neighborhood Prayer Walking

Eric and Stephanie have both worked on the ground helping Episcopalians to become conversation partners and companions with their neighborhoods. Once upon a time, clergy and lay leaders walked the "bounds" of their parishes, the geographic, physical area where God planted them. An ideal first step today may be a Neighborhood Prayer Walk (see the resource at www.episcopalchurch.org/evangelism for tips on leading such a walk). The idea is simple and works in a variety of contexts.

- Map the area where you will walk. It could be in a city, town, suburb or rural area. The point is to get to know the

---

* The Lambeth Conference 1968, *Resolutions and Reports* (New York: Seabury, 1968), 140.

neighborhood where God has called you to relationship and ministry as a neighbor. It may include a mall; a soccer field or playground on a Sunday right after church; a run-down street that once hosted thriving businesses; a dense apartment complex. The neighborhood is wherever your neighbors are.

• Gather a group from your ministry. Break into smaller groups of as few as two or three people, but no more than six. Don't talk and chat too much with each other. Instead, be fully present to what's around you. Notice the places where people gather, the languages on signs, the condition of schools, the places of energy and life, the places of desolation. Look for signs of physical, social, economic, spiritual, and ecological wellness, energy, and life. Also notice signs of unwellness and desolation.

• Take a few notes, but it is best not to carry a notebook and approach the walk as research. Your first goal is simply to be a prayerful presence and to ask God to open your eyes.

• In the course of the prayer walk, or in research afterward, you can get to know even more about the neighborhood. Who has power and privilege? Who appears to lack it? Where do you see economic status playing out? Are some people treated differently because of their age, gender identity, sexual orientation, mental or physical ability, medical or health status, race or language, or other identity markers?

• At the end of the walk, invite the walkers to gather and share their notes, reflections and prayers. Discuss similarities and differences.

- As a group, name up to three places where you noticed signs of wellness. Discern together with simple questions: How is God leading us to learn more, grow relationships and bless the wellness in the neighborhood? Do we already see ways to use our resources and assets to foster wellness in this place?

- Then name up to three places where you noticed signs of struggle or unwellness, and discern with the same questions: How is God leading us to learn more, grow relationships and join in healing and fostering wellness in the neighborhood? Do we already see ways to use our resources and assets to heal unwellness and grow wellness in this place?

You won't arrive at answers or a strategic plan immediately. That is because you are not walking the neighborhood with prefab notions of what you can do for "them" or what "they" need. If you do, you will find it more difficult to be fully open to God's prodding and revelation. Instead, allow the truth and perhaps more questions to unfold as you walk the neighborhood. Pay attention. Be curious. Don't judge or overlook things you don't want to see. Find out who lives in the neighborhood and what dreams, struggles, and issues concern them. Pray for a spirit of humility and curiosity before you even set out. Pray for new relationships and fresh insight. Then offer what you see to God, and ask God how you could engage and join what's happening, as both learners and healers and above all as partners. Let God—and your neighbors—tell you what conversations and relationships are waiting to happen here.

Next Steps on the Way

Eventually, you could expand the practice of Neighborhood Prayer Walks into other communities and areas. Some people do walks like these when they arrive in a new mission area, whether it is local or global. A Prayer Walk can be a helpful way to become aware as you enter any place where God is calling you or your church to stretch beyond itself.

Prayerful observation and learning is the foundation for real relationship. From that starting place, you can go out, be curious and humble, and find opportunities to meet the people you do not know and let them be your companions and guides. In the Gospel of Luke, Jesus offers his disciples these instructions for walking with their neighbors:

> After this the Lord appointed seventy others and sent them on ahead of him in pairs to every town and place where he himself intended to go. He said to them, "The harvest is plentiful, but the laborers are few; therefore ask the Lord of the harvest to send out laborers into his harvest. Go on your way. See, I am sending you out like lambs into the midst of wolves. Carry no purse, no bag, no sandals; and greet no one on the road. Whatever house you enter, first say, 'Peace to this house!' And if anyone is there who shares in peace, your peace will rest on that person; but if not, it will return to you. Remain in the same house, eating and drinking whatever they provide, for the laborer deserves to be paid. Do not move about from house to house. Whenever you enter a town and its people welcome you, eat what is set before you; cure the sick who are there, and say to them, 'The kingdom of God has come near to you.'" (Luke 10:1–9)

The followers of Jesus are gracious and curious. We follow the lead of our neighbors, listen deeply to what they reveal, and receive their gifts with joy, even as we share the healing and peace of God with them. And whenever we see the kingdom breaking in, we celebrate it.

Chapter 13

Walking and Talking with My Enemy

We live in a world conditioned by either/or thinking. Everything is either true or false, right or wrong, good or bad. Before long, we extend these judgments from the idea to a person or group. "I disagree with that idea" becomes "I disagree with you" becomes "You are wrong" and finally "You are my enemy."

Is there another way? How does anyone follow Jesus's command and actually love the enemy? Eric returns to the deep wisdom of Chinese and Hebrew traditions for help with this age-old struggle.

In Chinese, the word for truthful or genuine, 真 (zhēn), consists of the three ideograms: 十 (shí) and 目 (mù). 十 is the number ten, while 目 represents the eye. The bottom part of the word symbolizes a table. The number ten symbolizes completeness or wholeness. Put them together, and you see that discerning the truth requires looking at an issue or event in a holistic way, perhaps through ten different eyes or ten different perspectives placed on a table.

As he pointed out in *The Episcopal Way*, the Hebrew word for truth, *emet*, is composed of the three letters א-alef, מ-mem,

ת-tav—the first, middle, and last letters of the Hebrew alphabet. This could mean that, for something to be true, it must embrace the beginning, the middle, and the end.

From here, Jesus's call to love our enemies begins to make more practical sense. God's world includes myriad people, nations, cultures, languages, expressions, and ideas. The only way we get to what is true is if we listen to each other, even the voices we would prefer never to hear, especially the voice of the enemy. I love my enemy because I need him.

Beyond Either/Or

As we discussed in the previous chapter, this spirit of humility and comprehensiveness is at the heart of the Episcopal Way. Thanks to the Via Media, we are constantly challenged to step beyond either/or binaries. Technology is not always anti-nature. Globalism and localism are not mutually exclusive. Immigrants and citizens do not have to fear each other. Gay and straight are not a threat to one another. Democrats and Republicans are not instantly adversaries. Men and women are not opposites. As Archbishop Desmond Tutu once said, "Differences are not intended to separate, to alienate. We are different precisely in order to realize our need of one another."*

The Episcopal Way of discerning the truth invites us to take different perspectives into account, even when they seem to be opposite or contrary to each other. This forces us to listen deeply to voices, texts, perspectives, and traditions that have

---

* Desmond Tutu, *God Has a Dream: A Vision of Hope for Our Time* (New York, Doubleday Image Books, 2004), 76.

been privileged through history *and* to the ones that have been consistently ignored. It challenges us to ask not only what is true or loving but how did different people land where they did. It forces us to admit that we genuinely need this other person and their perspective in order to learn what is true, right, and good. I do not know the truth unless I am willing to

How do I actually walk and talk with the one with whom I most disagree? What if that person is a bully and abuser? What if they have no desire to enter the conversation with me?

see the issue or question from different perspectives, including the perspective of my enemy.

Laywoman and theologian Verna Dozier heard plenty of critics in her day who complained about this Episcopal habit of openness. In a 1997 interview, she said: "It is important to keep open to the possibility that I may be wrong. . . . I need to understand that where I stand is not necessarily the totality of where God stands."* In her classic *The Dream of God*, she expands on the same point:

> Doubt is not the opposite of faith: fear is. Fear will not risk that even if I am wrong, I will trust that if I move today by the light that is given me, knowing it is only finite and partial, I will know more and different things tomorrow than I know today, and I can be open to the new possibility I cannot even imagine today.**

---

* Verna Dozier, from an interview quoted in Richard Schmidt, *Glorious Companions: Five Centuries of Anglican Spirituality* (Grand Rapids, Michigan: Eerdmans, 2002), 297.

** Verna Dozier, *The Dream of God: A Call to Return* (1991; New York: Church Publishing, 2006), 47.

If it sounds complex and messy, it is. Dozier would be the first to warn that this way of walking may take more faith, not less, than simply deciding who is right and who is wrong and moving on. That is the cost of following the Episcopal Way and engaging in conversation with ten eyes on the table, conscious of the beginning, the middle, and the end.

Gracious Listening

These principles sound lovely when it's simply talk. How do I actually walk and talk with the one with whom I most disagree? What if that person is a bully and abuser? What if they have no desire to enter the conversation with me? Why would I put myself in that destructive situation? In the light of day, Jesus's charge to love our enemies looks like one more gospel imperative that we cannot hope to apply in the real world.

As we write this book, the divisions among Americans have in many places hardened to the point where we may not only disagree, but see others as enemies. Since the 2016 presidential election, we have heard a growing cry for help engaging in constructive, non-argumentative conversation across deep political and cultural divides. Everyone wants to know how to avoid a yelling match that generates more hurt and fear. Some resources are:

- "Beloved Community StorySharing Guidebook," a resource that trains people to share and receive others' stories about faith, race and difference. Find the guidebook and learn about others engaged in the practice of sharing stories and building Beloved Community at www.episcopalchurch.org/storysharing.

- "Civil Discourse Curriculum," a five-week program created by the Episcopal Church's Office of Government Affairs and the Formation Department. Available at www.advocacy .episcopalchuch.org/resources.

- Essential Partners' "Reaching Out Across the Red/Blue Divide," a resource created for *USA Today* newspaper. Available at https://www.whatisessential.org/sites/default/files/ Red-Blue%20Divide%20Guide.pdf.

Soon after the election, Eric created a resource for having reasonable, civil and even productive conversations. It was designed with electoral politics in mind, but we adapt and abbreviate it here to work for a wider range of conversations and conflicts (http://ehflaw.typepad.com/blog/2017/06/focus-on-what-really-matters-ii-building-one-bridge-at-a-time.html):

1. Prepare: Take some time to reflect on why you voted the way you did or why you believe what you do. What is the impact of this decision and the result on you personally, your family, your work, your friends, your community, etc. How has it affected others? Remember that you are claiming your own experience, not making a judgment or trying to convince anyone else. Try completing these sentences:

- I supported _____ because I _____.
- When the results came in, I _____.
- In light of what has occurred since the _____, I have experienced _____.
- Since the _____, I have been most concerned about _____.

2. Decide to engage: When it looks like you and your conversation partner are heading toward disagreement about politics or another contentious subject, make a decision whether this is "worth it." Why do you want to connect with this person? What do you want to learn? Are you genuinely curious about this person's experience? If your decision is that it is not worth your while, then steer the conversation differently or end it.

3. Agree on a time and place: If you want to have the conversation, decide whether this the right place and time for it. Eric offers these real-time queries:

- "I really want to talk with you about this. Can we go somewhere quiet and spend fifteen minutes having a real conversation?"

- "I really want to continue our conversation, but this is neither the time and place for it. Can we commit to getting together for half an hour for coffee or tea at a time and place that is convenient for both of us?"

4. Set parameters and ground rules: Before you start (or restart) the conversation, set guidelines for conversation. Eric has developed Respectful Communication Guidelines and shares them through the Kaleidoscope Institute (they are also featured on page 81 of *The Episcopal Way*). If pulling out a card or bookmark feels like a distraction, he offers this more conversational way to offer ground-rules:

First, invite the person to have an honest thoughtful conversation and not a debate about who is right or wrong. If your conversation partner cannot agree to this goal and to some guidelines for communication, it is best not to enter into the conversation.

If you have established the initial agreement, try offering these queries to move forward:

- "Can we agree to share our experiences and not try defend anyone else or a whole party?"

- "Can we agree not to be dismissive of each other's experiences? Can we not judge, blame, and shame each other?"

- "Can we not interrupt each other, and let each other finish our thoughts before responding?"

- "Can we agree to hang in there. even when we don't quite understand each other's perspective yet? If we're confused, can we ask clarifying questions of each other?"

5. Start with insightful questions: Do not begin with yes/no, right/wrong, good/bad questions. Start with information-seeking questions that help both of you to share your interests, values and beliefs. Try questions like these:

- What is most important to you in your (political/religious/general) beliefs?

- What life experiences have led you to believe what you do?

- What hopes, concerns, and values are at the heart of your beliefs?

Once you are able to share about values and beliefs, you can move into more specific questions about the contentious issue or event.

6. Ask for feedback and stay curious: The conversation may break down or get sidetracked for any number of reasons. Stop, take a deep breath and refocus by asking yourself questions like these:

- Am I really listening?
- Am I only listening to what I want to hear?
- Am I looking for faults in the other person?
- Am I trying to convince him/her to believe what I do?

Try returning to humility and curiosity. Remind yourself that the purpose of this conversation is not to agree but to understand. Let your conversation partner know that you are trying to understand by giving feedback and asking clarifying questions. Try these:

- "Let me make sure I understand what you mean. You are saying that this is important to you because _____. Is that right?"
- "How did you come to believe that?"
- "Was there an experience that led you to believe that?"
- "Can you tell me why _____ is important to you?"

7. Thank your conversation partner: When the conversation comes to a natural stopping place, be sure you've shared around questions that help you to move forward. It could be as simple as asking, "In what ways can we stay connected and even support each other, in spite of and maybe because of our differences?"

As you conclude, be sure you share what you have learned from this conversation and invite your partner to do the same. Then thank your partner for entering into exchange and being a companion to you. If appropriate, you may pray together and set another time to further the conversation.

The process above works for more than conversation about how you voted in a presidential election. The same seven steps can be just as helpful for preparing to engage in courageous, gracious conversation with people who are quite different from you or with whom you radically disagree.

After a while, courageous, gracious conversation like this becomes more than a strategy to avoid fault lines and pitched battles. It becomes part of your spiritual practice. Eric recently wrote a poem about what it has revealed to him:

If God loves me
And God loves you,
What happens when we disagree?
What are we gonna do?
What are we gonna do?

If I listen to you
And you listen to me,
In between your words and mine,
We may hear the Word of God divine.
If you walk with me
And I walk with you,
In between my way and yours,
We can find the sacred path
That leads to many gracious open doors

If I see what you see
And you see what I see,
In between your view and mine,
We may see the view of God's design.
If you know my fears
And I know your fears
In between my fears and yours,
We can build a place that's safe
Where justice reigns, with grace and not with wars.

If God loves me
And God loves you,
What happens when we disagree?
What are we gonna do?
What are we gonna do?

What will we do in the face of deep division and fear? Episcopalians, at our best, welcome the one who is different to be our companion and to illuminate what we are, what we do, and how we might live as children of God. Our truth does not need to be the sole or universal truth. By having courageous and gracious conversation on the way, we discover the greater truth and decide what we will do together to heal our communities and our world. The Episcopal Way of following Jesus can equip us to wrestle with some of life's most fundamental questions—and eventually to listen, walk, see, know, and love where it is hardest.

Conclusion

At the close of *The Episcopal Way*, we provided an extended list of the signs that you are walking the Episcopal path closer to God.* We claimed then and still believe that . . .

The Episcopal Way travels the **Via Media,** a balanced "both/and" path that holds complexity and seeming contradiction without losing its hold on faith and truth.

The Episcopal Way is **catholic and Protestant**, grounded in ancient sacrament and ordered prayer, yet willing to change to meet a changing world.

The Episcopal Way rests on the **three-legged stool** of Scripture, tradition, and reason, all of which Christians must heed if we're going to follow Jesus and live as extensions of his body in the world.

---

* Law and Spellers, 101–102.

The Episcopal Way is deeply **incarnational** and follows the God who loved creation enough to dwell among us in flesh and blood.

The Episcopal Way is **liturgical,** following ancient structures and common forms for worship even as we adapt to share the story of God in emerging cultures.

The Episcopal Way is **networked,** locally and globally, and draws us into a web of relationship with a rich past, a broad present, and an unknown future.

The Episcopal Way is **democratic,** valuing every baptized person as a minister of God, and setting out structures and ordered ministries in order to facilitate our shared ministries.

The Episcopal Way celebrates the **Vernacular Principle** by translating the gospel and traditions into the language and culture of people on the ground.

The Episcopal Way is a way of **reason** and **mystery,** trusting there is a time to use our God-given reason and a time to rest in awe and wonder.

The Episcopal Way is flexible and **adaptive,** no longer bound by the fear of change.

The Episcopal Way lifts up **beauty,** because it offers a taste of heaven and stirs us to go seek and serve the Christ who shines beautifully in all people.

The Episcopal Way is **generous,** embracing people of all backgrounds and inviting each of us to contribute for the sake of God's kingdom.

The Episcopal Way is **in love with God,** the God we meet in Scripture, tradition, and reason, in flesh, nature, poetry, art; in the whole creation that God has made and redeemed.

We encourage you to seek companions of every kind and to keep faithfully walking this Episcopal Way. Remain in conversation with one another and with the doctrine, history, theology, social witness, ethics, ministry, Scripture, and worship that our beloved tradition has nurtured for centuries. If you do this, you will find yourself seeking and creating a gracious environment for conversation and companionship in every part of your life, and you will be a true companion to others seeking a path closer to the heart of God.

Our sisters and brothers in South Africa often speak of "Ubuntu," a theology of interdependence that states "I am because we are." Perhaps the Episcopal statement might run, "I am because we pray, walk, and talk. I know what is true and good because I discover that in conversation with God, with myself, and with *all* of you."

May it be so. Amen.